THE YEARS

THE YEARS
ANNIE ERNAUX

Translated by
Alison L. Strayer

SEVEN STORIES PRESS
New York · Oakland · London

Seven Stories Press
140 Watts Street
New York, NY 10013
www.sevenstories.com/

Library of Congress Cataloging-in-Publication Data

Names: Ernaux, Annie, 1940- author. | Strayer, Alison L., translator.
Title: The years / Annie Ernaux ; translated by Alison L. Strayer.
Other titles: Années. English
Description: First edition. | New York : Seven Stories Press, 2017. | First published in French as Les Années (Paris : Gallimard, c2008).
Identifiers: LCCN 2017003723 (print) | LCCN 2017023091 (ebook) | ISBN 9781609807887 (E-book) | ISBN 9781609807870 (paperback)
Subjects: LCSH: Ernaux, Annie, 1940- | Authors, French--20th century--Biography. | BISAC: BIOGRAPHY & AUTOBIOGRAPHY / Personal Memoirs.
| HISTORY / Europe / France. | HISTORY / Social History.
Classification: LCC PQ2665.R67 (ebook) | LCC PQ2665.R67 Z4613 2017 (print) | DDC 843/.914 [B] --dc23
LC record available at https://lccn.loc.gov/2017003723

College professors and high school and middle school teachers may order free examination copies of Seven Stories Press titles. To order, fax on school letterhead to (212) 226-1411 or visit www.sevenstories.com.

Printed in the United States of America

9 8 7 6 5 4 3 2 1

All we have is our history, and it
does not belong to us.
—José Ortega y Gasset

Yes. They'll forget us. Such is our fate, there
is no help for it. What seems to us serious,
significant, very important, will one day be
forgotten or will seem unimportant. And it's
curious that we can't possibly tell what exactly
will be considered great and important, and
what will seem petty and ridiculous [. . .].
And it may be that our present life, which we
accept so readily, will in time seem strange,
inconvenient, stupid, not clean enough,
perhaps even sinful . . .
—Anton Chekhov

Translated from the Russian by Constance Garnett
(New York: Macmillan, 1916)

All the images will disappear.

—the woman who squatted to urinate in broad daylight, behind the shack that served coffee at the edge of the ruins in Yvetot, after the war, who stood, skirts lifted, to pull up her underwear and then returned to the café

—the tearful face of Alida Valli as she danced with Georges Wilson in the film *The Long Absence*

—the man passed on a Padua sidewalk in the summer of 1990, his hands tied at the shoulders, instantly summoning the memory of thalidomide, prescribed to pregnant women for nausea thirty years before, and of a joke people told later: an expectant mother knits the baby's layette while gulping thalidomide pills at regular intervals—a row, a pill, a row, a pill. A friend says in horror, Stop, don't you realize your baby may be born without arms, and the other answers, It's okay, I don't know how to knit sleeves anyway

—Claude Piéplu who leads a regiment of légionnaires, waving a flag in one hand and leading a goat with the other, in a film with Les Charlots

—the majesty of the elderly woman with Alzheimer's, who wore a flowered smock like all the residents of the old folks' home, but with a blue shawl over her shoulders, tirelessly pacing the corridors, haughty like the Duchess of Guermantes in the Bois de Boulogne, and who made you think of Céleste Albaret as she'd appeared one night on television with Bernard Pivot

—on an outdoor stage, the woman shut into a box pierced all the way through by men with silver spears—and emerging alive because it was a magic trick, called *The Martyrdom of a Woman*

—the mummies clothed in tattered lace, dangling from the walls of the Convento dei Cappuccini in Palermo

—Simone Signoret's face on the poster for *Thérèse Raquin*

—the shoe rotating on a pedestal in an André store, rue du Gros-Horloge in Rouen, the same phrase continuously scrolling around it—*With Babybotte, Baby trots and grows well*

—the stranger of Termini Station in Rome, who half lowered the blind of his first-class compartment and in profile, hidden from the waist up, dandled his sex for the young women in the train on the opposite track, who leaned against the railing, chins in hands

—the guy in a cinema ad for Païc Vaisselle dishwashing liquid, cheerfully breaking dirty dishes instead of washing them while an offscreen voice sternly intoned "That is not the solution!" and the fellow, gazing at the audience in despair, asked "But what is the solution?"

—the beach at Arenys de Mar, next to a railway line, the hotel guest who looked like Zappy Max

—the newborn flailed in the air like a skinned rabbit in the delivery room of the Clinique Caudéran Pasteur, found again half an hour later, dressed and sleeping on his side in a little bed, one hand outside, and the sheet pulled up to his shoulders

—the dashing figure of the actor Philippe Lemaire, married to Juliette Greco

—in a TV commercial, the father who hides behind his newspaper, trying in vain to toss a Picorette in the air and catch it in his mouth, like his little girl

—a house with an arbor of Virginia creeper, which was a hotel in the sixties, no. 90A, on the Zattere in Venice

—the hundreds of petrified faces, photographed by the authorities before deportation to the camps, on the walls of a room in the Palais de Tokyo, Paris, in the mid-1980s

—the lavatories built above the river, in the courtyard behind the house in Lillebonne, the feces mixed with paper gently borne away by the water that laps around them

—all the twilight images of the early years, the pools of light from a summer Sunday, images from dreams in which the dead parents come back to life, and you walk down unidentifiable roads

—the image of Scarlett O'Hara, who kills a Yankee soldier and drags him up the stairs, then runs through the streets of Atlanta in search of a doctor for Melanie, who is about to give birth

—of Molly Bloom, who lies next to her husband, remembering the first time a boy kissed her and she said yes yes yes

—of Elizabeth Drummond, murdered with her parents on a road in Lurs in 1952

—the images, real or imaginary, that follow us all the way to sleep

—the images of a moment, bathed in a light that is theirs alone

They will vanish all at the same time, like the millions of images that lay behind the foreheads of the grandparents, dead for half a century, and of the parents, also dead. Images in which we appeared as a little girl in the midst of beings who died before we were born, just as in our own memories our small children are there next to our parents and schoolmates.

And one day we'll appear in our children's memories, among their grandchildren and people not yet born. Like sexual desire, memory never stops. It pairs the dead with the living, real with imaginary beings, dreams with history.

Thousands of words will suddenly be deleted, the ones that were used to name things, faces, acts and feelings, to put the world in order, make the heart beat and the sex grow moist.

—slogans, graffiti in public toilets, on walls in the street, poems and dirty stories, titles

—anamnesis, epigone, noema, theoretical, the terms written in a notebook with their meanings so you didn't need to look them up each time

—turns of phrase that others used without a thought and which we doubted we'd ever be able to use, *il est indéniable que, force est de constater*

—dreadful sentences one should have forgotten, more tenacious than others due to the effort expended to suppress them, you look like a decrepit whore

—the words of men in bed at night, Do with me what you will, I am your thing

—to exist is to drink oneself without thirst

—what were you doing on September 11, 2001?

—*in illo tempore* at Mass on Sunday

—*vieux kroumir, faire du chambard, ça valait mille! tu es un petit ballot,** outdated expressions, heard again by chance, suddenly precious as objects lost and found again, and you wonder how they've been saved from oblivion

—the words forever bound to certain people, like catchwords, or to a specific spot on the N14 because a passenger happened to say them just as we were driving by, and we cannot pass that place again without the words leaping up like the buried water jets at the Summer Palace of Peter the Great, which spray when you walk across them

—the grammar book examples, quotes, insults, songs, sentences copied into notebooks when we were teens

—*l'abbé Trublet compilait, compilait, compilait*

—glory for a woman can only be the dazzling mourning of happiness

—our memory is outside us, in a rainy breath of time

---

* old geezer, make a hullabaloo, that was priceless! You little nincompoop!

—Perfection for a nun is to spend her life as a virgin and to die as a saint

—Saucy spoonerisms: the acrobats displayed some cunning stunts, the explorer puts his mess in the cashbox

—*it was a lucky charm, a little pig with a heart / that she bought at the market for a hundred sous / a hundred sous is a pittance, between me and you*

—*mon histoire c'est l'histoire d'un amour*

—can you *tirlipote* with a fork? Can you put a *schmilblick* in a baby bottle?

(I'm capable of the best and the worst, but at being the worst I'm the best! so if you're gay, why don't you laugh? I'll be brief, said King Pepin the Short and climbing out of the monster's belly, Jonas declared, you don't need to be a brain sturgeon to know that's dolphinitely no minnow—the puns heard a thousand times, which had ceased to amuse or amaze us long ago; hackneyed, only irritating, they served no purpose but to consolidate the family esprit de corps, and disappeared when the couple blew apart though still sprang to mind sometimes, incongruous, inappropriate outside of the former tribe—basically, all that remained of it, after years of separation)

—words that we are astonished ever existed—*mastoc*, hefty (Flaubert in a letter to Louise Colet), *pioncer*, to kip down

(George Sand to Flaubert)!

—Latin and English. Russian learned in six months for a Soviet—nothing left of it now—*da svidania, ya tebia lioubliou kharacho*

—what is marriage? A con-promise

—metaphors so tired, we were astonished when others dared to utter them, the icing on the cake

—O Mother buried outside the first garden

—*pédaler à côté du vélo*, to pedal next to the bicycle (wasted effort) became *pédaler dans la choucroûte*, to pedal in sauerkraut (go nowhere fast), then in semolina (go in circles, spin one's wheels), then nothing—obsolete expressions

—the men's words we didn't like, *come, jerk off*

—the ones learned at school that gave you a feeling of mastery over the world. Once the exam was over, they flew out of your head more quickly than they had entered

—the repeated phrases of grandparents that set one's teeth on edge, and those of the parents which after their deaths remained more alive than their faces, *curiosity killed the cat, little jugs have big ears*

—the old brands, short-lived, the memories of which delighted you more than those of better-known brands, Dulsol shampoo,

Cardon chocolate, Nadi coffee—like an intimate memory, impossible to share

—*The Cranes Are Flying*

—*Marianne of My Youth*

—Madame Soleil is still with us

—The world is suffering from lack of faith in a transcendental truth

Everything will be erased in a second. The dictionary of words amassed between cradle and deathbed, eliminated. All there will be is silence and no words to say it. Nothing will come out of the open mouth, neither I nor me. Language will continue to put the world into words. In conversation around a holiday table, we will be nothing but a first name, increasingly faceless, until we vanish into the vast anonymity of a distant generation.

It is a sepia photo, oval-shaped, glued inside a little cardboard folder with a gold border and protected by a sheet of embossed, semitransparent paper. Below are the words: *Photo-Moderne, Ridel, Lillebonne (S.Inf.re)*. Tel. 80. A fat baby with a full, pouty lower lip and brown hair pulled up into a big curl sits half-naked on a cushion in the middle of a carved table. The misty background, the sculpted garland of the table, the embroidered chemise that rides up over the belly (the baby's hand hides its sex), the strap slipping from the shoulder onto the chubby arm suggest a cupid or a cherub from a painting. All the relatives must have received a print and immediately tried to discern whose side the child took after. In this piece of family archives, which must date from 1941, it is impossible not to read a ritual petit bourgeois staging for the entrance into the world.

Another photo, stamped by the same photographer—the folder is of lesser quality, the gold border has disappeared—and probably destined for the same distribution within the family, shows a little girl of about four, serious, almost sad despite her nice plump face under short hair, parted down the middle and pulled back with barrettes to which little bow-ties are attached, like butterflies. Her left hand rests on the same carved Louis XVI–style table, which is fully visible. She bulges out of her bodice, her skirt with shoulder straps hiked up a little over a protuberant belly, possibly a sign of rickets (circa 1944).

Two other small photos with serrated edges, very likely taken the same year, show the same child, slimmer, in a flounced dress with puff sleeves. In the first one, she nestles playfully against a stout woman, whose body is a solid mass in a wide-striped dress, her hair swept up in two big buns. In the other photo, the child's left hand is raised, fist closed, the right one held back by the hand of a man. He is tall with a light-colored jacket and pleated trousers, his bearing nonchalant. Both photos were taken on the same day in a cobbled courtyard, in front of a low wall with a floral border along the top. A clothesline hangs above their heads, a clothespin still hooked over it.

On holiday afternoons after the war, amidst the interminable slowness of meals, it appeared out of nowhere and took shape, the time already begun, the one which the parents seemed to be staring at, eyes unfocused, when they forgot to answer us, the time where we were not and never would be, the time before. The voices of the guests flowed together to compose the great narrative of collective events, which we came to believe we too had witnessed.

They never grew tired of talking about the winter of '42, the bone-chilling cold, the hunger and the rutabagas, the food provisions and tobacco vouchers, the bombardments

—the aurora borealis that heralded the coming of the war

—the bicycles and carts on the roads during the Rout, the looted shops

—the victims searching the debris for their photos and their money

—the arrival of the Germans—every person at the table could say exactly *where*, in what city, they'd landed—and the English, always courteous, the Americans, inconsiderate, the neighbor in the Resistance, the *collabos*, the girl X whose head was shaved after Liberation

—Le Havre razed to the ground and where nothing at all remained, the black market

—Propaganda

—the Boches fleeing across the Seine at Caudébec on broken-down horses

—the countrywoman who loudly broke wind in a train compartment full of Germans and proclaimed to all and sundry, "If we can't tell it, we'll make them smell it!"

From a common ground of hunger and fear, everything was told in the "we" voice and with impersonal pronouns.

Shrugging their shoulders, they spoke of Pétain, too old and already gaga when he was brought back into action, *faute de mieux*. They imitated the flight and rumble of V-2s circling above, mimed past terrors, feigning their own careful deliberations at critical moments, *What do I do now*, to keep us in suspense.

It was a story replete with violence, destruction, and death, narrated with glee, belied at intervals, it seemed, by a stirring and solemn "It must never happen again," followed by a silence like a warning for the benefit of some obscure authority, remorse in the wake of pleasure.

But they only spoke of what they had seen and could re-live while eating and drinking. They lacked the talent and conviction to speak of things they'd been aware of but had not seen. Therefore, no Jewish children boarding trains for Auschwitz, nor bodies of starvation victims collected every morning from the Warsaw Ghetto, nor Hiroshima's 10,000 degrees. Whence our impression, which later history courses, documentaries, and films failed to dispel, that neither the crematoria nor the atomic bomb belonged to the same timeline as black market butter, air-raid warnings, and descents to the cellar.

They started to make comparisons with the other war, 1914, the Great War, won in blood and glory, a man's war, and around the table the women listened to the men with respect. They spoke of Chemin des Dames and Verdun, the gassed soldiers, the bells of November 11, 1918. They named villages whose children left for the Front, never to return, not one. They compared the soldiers in the mud-filled trenches with the prisoners of 1940, warm and sheltered for five years without a bomb ever landing on them. They quarreled over who had been more heroic and who more unlucky.

They traveled back to times before their own existence, the Crimean War and the siege of 1870, when the Parisians ate rats.

In the time-before of which they spoke, there was nothing but war and hunger.

They finished by singing *Ah le petit vin blanc* and *Fleur de Paris*, shouting the refrain, *bleu-blanc-rouge sont les couleurs de la patrie* in a deafening chorus. They stretched their arms and laughed, *Here's another one the Boches won't get!*

The children didn't listen. They rushed from the table the moment they were excused and took advantage of the holiday goodwill to play forbidden games, jumping on beds, swinging upside down. But they remembered every detail. Next to that wondrous time, the episodes whose order they would not retain for years, the Rout, the Occupation, the Exodus, the Landing, the Victory, the nameless time in which they grew seemed colorless. They regretted they had not been born (or were only infants) in the days when people were forced to take to the roads in bands and sleep on straw like gypsies. Not having lived this way would stamp them with a lasting sorrow. They were saddled with other people's memories and a secret nostalgia for the time they'd missed by so little, along with the hope of living it one day.

All that remained of the flamboyant epic were the gray and silent ruins of blockhouses carved into cliffsides, and heaps of rubble in the towns as far as the eye could see. Rusty objects, twisted bedframes loomed out of the debris. Merchants who had lost their businesses set up shop in temporary huts along the edges of the ruins. Shells overlooked by mine-clearers exploded in the bellies of the little boys who played with them. The newspapers warned, Do not touch munitions! Doctors removed tonsils from children with delicate throats, who woke screaming from the ether anesthesia and were forced to drink boiling milk. On faded posters, General de Gaulle, in three-quarter profile, gazed into the distance from under his kepi. On Sunday afternoons we played Ludo and Old Maid.

The frenzy that had followed Liberation was fading. All that people thought about was going out, and the world was full of desires that clamored for immediate satisfaction. Anything that comprised a *first time since the war* provoked a stampede—bananas, fireworks, National Lottery tickets. Entire neighborhoods, from elderly ladies propped up by their daughters to infants in strollers, flocked to the funfair, the torchlight tattoo, and the Bouglione circus, where they narrowly escaped being crushed in the melee. They took to the road in praying, singing crowds to welcome the statue of Our Lady of Boulogne and walk her back the following day over many kilometers. They never missed a chance, secular or religious, to be outside with other people, as if they still yearned to live in a group. On Sunday evenings, the coaches returned from the seaside with tall youths in shorts clinging to the luggage roofs and singing at the top of their voices. Dogs roamed free and mated in the middle of the streets.

But even this time started to become a memory of golden days, whose loss we keenly felt when the radio played *Je me souviens des beaux dimanches . . . Mais oui c'est loin c'est loin tout ça.* Then the children began to regret having been too small to really experience the Liberation.

Still, we grew up quietly, "happy to be alive and see the world as it is," amidst the recommendations not to touch unknown objects and the ceaseless bemoaning of rationing, oil and sugar coupons, corn bread that sat heavy on the stomach, coke that didn't heat, and *will there be chocolate and jam for Christmas?* We started going to school with slates and chalk-holders, passing fields that had been cleared of debris and leveled for reconstruction. We played Drop the Handkerchief and Pass the Ring, danced in the round while singing *Bonjour Guillaume as-tu bien déjeuné*, played fives against the wall to *Petite bohémienne toi qui voyages partout*, and tramped up and down the schoolyard arm-in-arm chanting *who is going to play hide-and-seek*. We caught scabies and head lice that we smothered with towels doused in Marie Rose antiparasitic. One after the other, we clambered into the TB X-ray truck, keeping our coats and mufflers on. We spent the first medical visit giggling with shame to be wearing only panties in a room not in the least warmed by the flitting blue flame in a dish of methylated spirits on the table by the nurse. Soon, for the very first Youth Day, dressed in white from head to toe, we would march through the streets to the racetrack, cheered by the crowd. Between the sky and the wet grass, to the music that blared from the loudspeakers, together we would execute the *group gymnastics set* with a sense of grandeur and solitude.

The speeches said we represented the future.

From the polyphonic clangor of holiday meals, before the quarrels began with eternal enmities sworn, another great story emerged in fragments, intertwined with the one about war: the story of origins.

Men and women began to appear, some nameless except for a kinship title, "father," "grandfather," "great-grandmother," reduced to a character trait, a funny or tragic anecdote, the Spanish flu, the embolism, or kick from a horse that carried them off—and children who hadn't lived to be our age, a multitude of characters we'd never know. Over years, and with no small effort, the tangled threads of family were unraveled, until at last the "two sides" could be clearly distinguished, the people who were something to us by blood from those who were "nothing."

Family narrative and social narrative are one and the same. The voices around the table mapped out the territories of youth: countrysides and farms where, for time immemorial, men had been hired hands and girls housemaids; the factory where they all had met, stepped out together, and married, the small businesses to which the most ambitious had risen. They told stories that contained no personal detail except for births, weddings, and funerals, no travel except to regiments in distant garrison towns, existences entirely filled by work, its harsh conditions, the perils of drink. School was a mythical backdrop, a brief golden age with the schoolmaster as its rough god, equipped with an iron ruler for the rapping of knuckles.

The voices imparted a legacy of poverty and deprivation that long pre-dated the war and the restrictions. They plunged us into a timeless night, "a bygone era," and rhymed off its pleasures and difficulties, customs and practical wisdom:
—living in a house with a dirt floor
—wearing galoshes
—playing with a rag doll
—washing clothes in wood ash
—sewing a little pouch of garlic inside children's nightshirts near the navel to rid them of worms
—obeying parents and getting boxed on the ears anyway, *just think if I'd given them lip!*

Drew up an inventory of ignorances, yesterday's unknowns and nevers:
—red meat, oranges
—social security, the family allowance, and retirement at sixty-five
—vacations

Recalled the sources of pride—the strikes of 1936, the Popular Front, *before that, the worker counted for nothing*

We, the little people, back at the table for dessert, stayed to listen to the risqué tales that in the atmosphere of postprandial ease, the assembly ceased to hold in check, forgetting young ears. Songs of the parents' youth told of Paris and girls who fell into streams, gigolos and gigolettes, hoodlums who lurked at the city gates, *Le Grand Rouquin, L'Hirondelle du faubourg, Du gris que l'on prend dans ses doigts et qu'on roule*, songs of passion and pathos to which the singer, eyes closed, gave her entire body, and all around the table, tears were dabbed away with the corners of napkins. Then it was our turn to melt the company's hearts with *Étoile des neiges*.

Darkened photos passed from hand to hand, the backs soiled by all the other fingers that had handled them at other meals, coffee and fat dissolved into an indefinable hue. No one recognized their parents—or anyone, come to that—in the stiff and somber newly-weds, the wedding guests in tiered rows along a wall. Nor did one see oneself in the half-naked baby of indistinct sex, who sat on a cushion, an alien creature from a mute and inaccessible time.

After the war, at the never-ending table of holiday meals, amidst the laughter and exclamations, *our time will come soon enough, let's enjoy it while it lasts,* other people's memories gave us a place in the world.

Memory was transmitted not only through the stories but through the ways of walking, sitting, talking, laughing, eating, hailing someone, grabbing hold of objects. It passed body to body, over the years, from the remotest countrysides of France and other parts of Europe: a heritage unseen in the photos, lying beyond individual difference and the gaps between the goodness of some and the wickedness of others. It united family members, neighbors, and all those of whom one said "They're people like us," a repertory of habits and gestures shaped by childhoods in the fields and teen years in workshops, preceded by other childhoods, all the way back to oblivion:

—eating noisily and displaying the progressive metamorphosis of food in the open mouth, wiping one's lips with a piece of bread, mopping the gravy from a plate so thoroughly that it could be put away without washing, tapping the spoon on the bottom of the bowl, stretching at the end of dinner. Daily washing of the face only, the rest according to the degree of soiling—hands and forearms after work, the legs and knees of children on summer evenings—and saving the big scrub-downs for holidays

—grabbing hold of things with force, slamming doors. Doing everything roughly, whether catching a rabbit by the ears, giving someone a peck on the cheek, or squeezing a child in one's arms. On days when tempers flared, banging in and out of the house, slamming chairs around

—walking with long strides, swinging one's arms, sitting by flopping oneself onto the chair, and when standing again, freeing with a flick of the hand the cloth of the skirt caught between the buttocks. Old women sat by pushing a fist into the hollow of the apron

—for men, the continual use of the shoulders in carrying a spade, planks, sacks of potatoes, and tired children on the way home from the fair

—for women, wedging things between the knees and thighs: the coffee grinder, the bottle to uncork, the hen whose throat is to be cut and whose blood will drip into a basin

—speaking loudly and grudgingly in every circumstance, as if one were forever obliged to bridle against the universe

The language, a mangled French mixed with local dialect, was inseparable from the hearty booming voices, bodies squeezed into work smocks and blue overalls, single-story houses and little gardens, dogs that barked in the afternoon and the silence that preceded arguments, just as the rules of grammar and proper French were associated with the neutral intonations and white hands of the schoolmistress. A language without praise or flattery that contained the piercing rain, the beaches of flat gray stones beneath sheer cliffs, the night buckets emptied onto manure, the wine drunk by laborers. It served as a vehicle for beliefs and prescriptions:

—observe the moon, for it governs the time of birth, the lifting of leeks, and the unpleasant routine for treating children's worms

—do not defy the cycle of the seasons to abandon coats and stockings, put the female rabbit to the male, or plant lettuces; there's a right time for everything, a precious interval between "too early" and "too late," difficult to quantify, when nature exerts her goodwill; children and cats born in winter don't grow as well as others, and the sun in March can drive one insane

—apply raw potato to burns, or "get the fire put out" by a neighbor who knows the magic formula; heal a cut with urine

—respect bread, for the face of God is etched on every grain of wheat

Like any language, this one created hierarchies, stigmatized slackers, unruly women, underhanded children, "satyrs" and "wastes of space," praised "capable" people and industrious girls, recognized bigwigs and higher-ups, admonished, *life will cut you down to size!*

It expressed reasonable desires and expectations: clean work, an indoor workplace, enough to eat, dying in bed

—limits: don't ask for the moon or things that cost the earth, be happy with what you've got
—the dread of departures and the unknown because when you never leave home, even the next town is the ends of the earth
—pride and injury, *just because we're from the country doesn't mean we're stupid*

But unlike our parents, we didn't miss school to plant colza, shake apples from trees, or bundle dead wood. The school calendar had replaced the cycle of the seasons. The years ahead were school years, stacked on top of each other, space-times that opened in October and closed in July. When school started, we folded blue paper covers over the used books bequeathed to us by pupils a grade ahead. When we looked at their poorly erased names on the cover pages, and the words they'd underlined, we felt as if we had taken over for them, and they were cheering us on—they who had made it through, learned all those things in a year. We memorized poems by Maurice Rollinat, Jean Richepin, Emile Verhaeren, Rosamond Gérard, and songs, *Mon beau sapin roi des forêts, C'est lui le voilà le dimanche avec sa robe de mai nouveau*. We applied ourselves to making zero mistakes on dictations from the works of Maurice Genevoix, La Varende, Émile Moselly, Ernest Pérochon. We recited the grammar rules of correct French. Then as soon as we got home, without a second thought, we reverted to the original tongue, which didn't force us to think about words but only things to say and not say—the language that clung to the body, was linked to slaps in the face, the Javel water smell of work coats, baked apples all winter long, the sound of piss in the night bucket, and the parents' snoring.

People's deaths didn't affect us at all.

The black-and-white photo of a little girl in a dark swimsuit on a pebble beach. In the background, cliffs. She sits on a flat rock, sturdy legs stretched out very straight in front of her. She leans back on her arms, smiling, eyes closed, her head slightly tilted. One thick brown braid has been arranged in front, the other hangs down her back. These details reveal the desire to pose like the stars in *Cinémonde* or the ads for Ambre Solaire, to flee her humiliating and unimportant little-girl body. Her thighs, paler, like her upper arms, show the outlines of a dress and indicate that for this child, a holiday or an afternoon at the seaside are exceptions to the rule. The beach is deserted. Written on the back: *August 1949, Sotteville-sur-Mer.*

She is about to turn nine, on holiday with her father, and her uncle and aunt who work at the rope factory. Her mother has remained in Yvetot to run the café-grocery, which never closes. Usually it is she who braids the girl's hair in two tight plaits and secures them, coronet-style, around her head, with spring barrettes and ribbons. It may be that neither her father nor her aunt knows how to pin up her braids, or that she's taking advantage of her mother's absence to let them down.

It is difficult to say what the girl is thinking or dreaming, and how she looks upon the years that have passed since the Liberation, which she remembers without effort.

Maybe the images have already fled, except for the ones that will always resist loss of memory:

—their arrival in the town reduced to rubble, the bitch in heat running away

—the first day of school after Easter, and she doesn't know anyone

—the great expedition to Fécamp on a train with wooden benches, the entire family on her mother's side; the grandmother wears a black rice straw hat, the cousins undress, bare-bottomed on the pebble beach

—the hoof-shaped needle case made for Christmas with a scrap of shirt cloth

—*Pas si bête* with Bourvil

—secret games, pinching the earlobes with toothed curtain rings.

Maybe she is gazing at the school years behind her, like a vast plain—the three grades she's passed, the arrangement of the little desks, the one big desk for the teacher, the chalkboard, the schoolmates:

—Françoise C, whom she envies for playing the clown with her hat in the shape of a cat's head, who asked to borrow her handkerchief once during recess, blew her nose into it thickly, handed it back in a ball, and ran away; her feeling of defilement and shame with the soiled handkerchief in her coat pocket for all of recess

—Évelyne J, whose hand she grabbed under the desk and stuck down her underpants, making her touch the sticky little ball

—F, whom no one ever talked to, sent to a sanatorium; at the medical exam she wore boy's underpants, stained with caca, and all the girls watched her, giggling

—the summers from before, already distant; one a scorcher, when the cisterns and wells ran dry, neighborhood people with jugs lined up at the fire hydrant, and Robic had won the Tour de France—another summer, rainy, when she collected mussels with her mother and aunt on the beach of Veules-les-Roses and they leaned over a hole in the cliff to see a dead soldier being dug up along with others, to be buried somewhere else

Unless she has preferred, as usual, to combine the many imaginary possibilities borrowed from the *Bibliothèque Verte* or the *Suzette* serials with the dream of her future, as she feels it inside when she hears a love song on the radio.

There is probably nothing on her mind that has to do with political events, crimes, random news items, and all that will later be acknowledged to have shaped the landscape of her child-hood—a set of things known and "in the air," Vincent Auriol, the war in Indochina, Marcel Cerdan, boxing champion of the world, *Pierrot le fou*, and Marie Besnard the arsenic poisoner.

Nothing is certain but her desire to be grown-up, and the absence of the following memory:
—that of the first time they said, before the photo of the baby on the cushion in a nightdress, and others, identical, oval-shaped and sepia, "That's you," forcing her to see herself in that other, shaped from chubby flesh, who'd lived a mysterious life in a time that no longer existed.

France was immense, composed of populations distinguished by the food they ate and their ways of speaking. In July, the riders of the Tour cycled across the country, and we followed them stage by stage on the Michelin map tacked onto the kitchen wall. Most people spent their lives within the same fifty kilometers, and when the church trembled with the first triumphal bars of the hymn "In Our Home Be Queen," we knew that *home* meant the place we lived, the town, or at most the *département*. The gateway to the exotic was the nearest big town, the rest of the world unreal. Those who were, or aspired to be, well educated enrolled in the *Connaissance du monde* documentary lectures. The others read *Reader's Digest* or *Constellation*, "the world seen in French." A postcard sent from Bizerte by a cousin doing his military service in Tunisia threw us into a state of moony, mute amazement.

Paris was beauty and power, a mysterious, frightening entity whose every street name that appeared in a newspaper or an ad—Boulevard Barbès, rue Gazan, Jean Mineur, 116 avenue des Champs-Élysées—inflamed the imagination. People who had lived or even just visited there and seen the Eiffel Tower took on an aura of superiority. On summer evenings, after the long and dusty days of vacation, we went to the station to meet the express trains and watch the people who'd been someplace else. We saw them disembark with suitcases and Printemps shopping bags, pilgrims returning from Lourdes. Songs about unknown places, the South, the Pyrenées—*Fandangos du pays basque, Montagnes d'Italie, Mexico*—made us yearn. In the pink-rimmed clouds of sunset, we saw maharajahs and Indian palaces. We complained to our parents, "We never go anywhere!" and they replied, astonished, "Where do you want to go, you've got all you need right here!"

Everything inside the houses had been bought before the war. The saucepans were blackened and missing their handles, the bowls' enamel worn away. Holes in jugs were plugged with metal pellets. Coats were revamped, shirt collars turned inside out, and Sunday clothes extended to everyday. That we never stopped growing made our mothers despair, forced to lengthen dresses with strips of cloth. Shoes bought a size up were too small the following year. Everything had to be put to use, the pen case, the Lefranc paint box, the packaging from LU Petit Beurre biscuits. Nothing was thrown away. The contents of night buckets were used for garden fertilizer, the dung of passing horses collected for potted plants. Newspaper was used for wrapping vegetables, drying shoes, wiping one's bottom in the lavatory.

We lived in a scarcity of everything, of objects, images, diversions, explanations of self and the world, whose sources were confined to the catechism, Father Riquet's sermon for Lent, the *Latest News from Tomorrow*, read in the booming voice of Geneviève Tabouis, and women's stories about their lives and those of their neighbors, exchanged over glasses of coffee in the afternoon. For the longest time, children believed in Santa Claus and babies found in roses or heads of cabbage.

People traveled by foot or bicycle in a smooth, regular motion. Men rode with their knees splayed and trouser cuffs cinched with clips, women with their bottoms encased in taut skirts, drawing fluid lines in the tranquillity of the streets. The background was silence and the bicycle measured the speed of life.

We lived in close proximity to shit. It made us laugh.

There were dead children in every family, carried off by sudden incurable diseases: diarrhea, convulsions, diphtheria. All that remained of their brief time on earth were tombstones shaped like baby cribs and inscribed "an angel in heaven." There were photos that people showed while furtively wiping their eyes, and hushed, almost serene conversations that frightened surviving children, who believed they were living on borrowed time. They would not be safe until the age of twelve or fifteen, having made it through whooping cough, measles, chicken pox, mumps, ear infections, and bronchitis every winter, escaped tuberculosis and meningitis, at which time people would say they'd "filled out." In the meantime, "war children," peaky and anemic with white-spotted nails, had to swallow cod-liver oil and Lune deworming syrup, chew Jessel tablets, step on the chemist's scale, bundle themselves in mufflers to avoid chills, eat soup for growth, and stand up straight under threat of wearing an iron corset. The babies who were starting to be born in every direction were vaccinated, monitored, and presented each month at the town hall's infant weigh-in. Newspaper headlines proclaimed that five thousand of them still died each year.

Idiocy from birth frightened no one. Madness was feared because it happened suddenly, mysteriously, to normal people.

The blurred and damaged photo of a little girl standing on a bridge in front of a guardrail. She has short hair, slender thighs, and knobby knees. She holds her hand over her eyes to block the sun. She is laughing. Written on the back of the photo, *Ginette 1937*. On her tombstone: *died at the age of six on Holy Thursday, 1938.* She is the older sister of the little girl on the beach at Sotteville-sur-Mer.

Boys and girls were kept apart in every situation. Boys were noisy creatures who never cried and were always ready to throw something—pebbles, chestnuts, firecrackers, tight-packed snowballs. They said bad words, read *Tarzan* and *Bibi Fricotin*. The girls, who feared them, were enjoined not to follow their example and to prefer quiet games like Pass the Ring, hopscotch, and dancing in the round. On Thursdays in winter, they taught school to old buttons or cutout figures from *L'Écho de la Mode* laid out on the kitchen table. The mothers and the school encouraged them to snitch. Their favorite threat was, "I'm telling on you!" They called out to each other *Hey, whatsyername,* listened to rude stories and repeated them in whispers, hands cupped over their mouths. They laughed up their sleeves at the story of Maria Goretti, who had preferred to die rather than do with a boy what they all longed to do. They frightened themselves with their lechery, which adults would never have dreamed possible. They longed to have breasts and body hair, a blood-stained towel between their legs. In the meantime, they read albums from the *Bécassine* series and *Hans Brinker or The Silver Skates* by P.-J. Stahl, and *Nobody's Boy* by Hector Malot. They went to the cinema with the school to see *Monsieur Vincent*, *Le grand cirque*, and *The Battle of the Rails*, which elevated the soul, boosted moral courage, and drove away wicked thoughts. As for reality and the future, those were to be found (they knew) in the films of Martine Carol and the photo-romance magazines, whose titles—*Nous Deux*, *Confidences*, and *Intimité*—foretold the alluring, illicit immorality that lay ahead.

The buildings of the reconstruction rose from the earth amidst the intermittent screech of pivot cranes. The days of restrictions were at an end, and new products appeared at long-enough intervals to be greeted with joyous surprise. Their utility was assessed and debated in daily conversation. They materialized suddenly, as in fairy tales, unprecedented, impossible to foresee. There was something for everyone, Bic pens, shampoo in pyramid-shaped cartons, Bulgomme bubble gum, Gerflex, Tampax, and creams to remove unwanted hair, Gilac plastics, Dacron, neon tubes, hazelnut milk chocolate, the Solex motorbike, chlorophyll toothpaste. We were continually amazed by the amount of time we saved with instant powdered soup, Presto pressure cookers, and mayonnaise in tubes. Canned was preferred to fresh, peas from tins instead of garden-picked. It was considered more chic to serve pears in syrup than ripe from the tree. Food's "digestibility," vitamins, and "calorie count" had started to matter. We marveled at inventions that erased centuries of gestures and effort. Soon would come a time, so it was said, when there'd be nothing left for us to do. Inventions were denigrated. The washing machine was accused of wearing out clothes, television of ruining the eyes and inciting people to stay up all hours. Still, we observed and envied our neighbors for possessing these signs of progress and social superiority. In the city, older boys on Vespas wheeled around the girls. Straight and proud in the saddle, they'd carry one off, a scarf tied under her chin, her arms twined around his back. We immediately wanted to be three years older, watching them ride off in a series of backfires.

Advertising touted the virtues of objects with commanding enthusiasm. *Furniture by Lévitan—guaranteed to last! Chantelle, the girdle that never rides up! You'll always prefer oil by Lesieur!* It sang them out with unbridled joy: *Dop dop dop, adopt Dop shampoo, Izarra la la li la li la, Apo po apopo Apollinaris,* or dreamily, *There's happiness in the home when* Elle *is there.* It crooned with the voice of Luis Mariano, *The brassiere by Lou, for the woman of bon goût.* While we did our homework at the kitchen table, the ads on Radio Luxembourg, like the songs, brought certainty of future joy, and all around us we felt the presence of absent things we'd be allowed to buy later. Meanwhile, as we waited to be old enough to wear Rouge Baiser lipstick and perfume by Bourjois *with a j as in joy*, we collected plastic animals hidden in bags of coffee, and from Menier chocolate wrappers, *Fables of La Fontaine* stamps that we swapped with friends at recess.

We had time to desire things, plastic pencil cases, crepe-soled shoes, gold watches. Their possession did not disappoint. We held them up to the admiration of others. They contained a mystery and magic that survived their contemplation and handling. Turning them this way and that, we continued to expect we-didn't-quite-know-what.

Progress was the bright horizon of every existence. It signified well-being, healthy children, glowing houses, well-lighted streets, and knowledge—everything that shunned the darkness of country life and the war. It was in plastics and Formica, antibiotics and social security benefits, running water and sewer lines, summer camps, ongoing education, and the atom. *You have to keep up with the times*, people liked to repeat, as proof of their intelligence and open minds. Eighth-grade composition topics invited students to write about "the benefits of electricity" or compose a reply to "someone who denigrates the modern world in your presence." *The young will know far more about it than us*, parents asserted.

In reality, cramped housing forced children and parents, brothers and sisters to sleep in the same room. People used jugs and basins to wash, did their business in outhouses. Sanitary napkins were made of toweling and left to disgorge their blood in buckets of icy water. Children's colds and bronchitis were treated with mustard poultices. Parents treated their own flu with Aspro and grog. Men pissed along the walls in broad daylight. Education aroused suspicion, a fear that through some obscure sanction, a punitive reversal that awaited those who tried to rise too high, learning made you lose your marbles. Teeth were missing from every mouth. The times, people said, are not the same for everyone.

The days passed unchanged, punctuated by the same old distractions, which could not keep pace with the abundance and novelty of *things*. Spring brought the return of First Communions, Youth Day, the church bazaar, and the Pinder Circus parade, when all at once the elephants blocked the street with their gray immensity. July was the Tour de France, which we followed on the radio, cutting photos from the papers—Geminiani, Darrigade, and Coppi—and pasting them in albums. Autumn brought the fair with midway rides and concessions. We rode the bumper cars enough to last us a year, amidst the clatter of metal rods, volleys of sparks, and a voice that boomed, "Here we go, boys and girls—three, two, one!" Year after year, on the lottery stage, the same boy with a red-painted nose imitated Bourvil, and a woman hawker, cleavage bared to the cold, reeled off her sales pitch for "Folies Bergère from midnight till two," a torrid show restricted to those sixteen and over. We searched for clues in the faces of people who had dared go behind the curtain and came out grinning. In the odor of stagnant water and animal fat, we sensed unbridled lust.

Later, we would be old enough to lift the tent flap. Behind it, three women in bikinis danced without music on a wooden stage. The lights went off and on again. The women stood bare-breasted and motionless in front of a sparse audience standing on the asphalt in front of the town hall. Outside, a loudspeaker bellowed a song by Dario Moreno, *Hey mambo, mambo italiano.*

Religion provided the official framework of life and governed Time. The newspapers published menus for Lent, whose stages from Septuagesima to Easter were marked on the calendar from La Poste. We didn't eat meat on Fridays. Sunday Mass remained an opportunity to change clothes, wear a garment for the first time, put on a hat and gloves, carry a purse, see and be seen, gaze at the altar boys. It was, for everyone, an outward sign of morality and the promise of a destiny, written in a special language, Latin. To read the same prayers each week, endure the same ritual boredom during the sermons, granted us probationary purification from pleasures such as eating chicken and bakeshop cakes, or going to a movie later. That schoolteachers and educated people, of irreproachable conduct, believed in nothing seemed an anomaly. Religion was the sole font of morality. It bestowed human dignity, without which our lives would resemble those of dogs. Church Law outweighed all others; it alone gave legitimacy to the great moments of existence. "People who don't marry in the Church are not really married," the catechism proclaimed. By "Church" they meant the Catholic Church, of course. All other religions were ridiculous or simply wrong. In the playground we bawled, *Mohammed was a prophet of the great Allah, / He sold peanuts at the market of Biskra. / Cotton candy would've been dandy / But he sells peanuts, that's all! / Allah* (three times).

We couldn't wait to do our Solemn Communion, the glorious precursor of everything important that would happen to us: periods, the certificate of education, entry into twelfth grade. Boys and girls sat separately in pews on either side of the aisle. The boys wore dark suits with armbands, the girls long white dresses and veils. We already looked like the husbands and wives we'd be in ten years' time, gliding two by two. Having thundered in a single voice at vespers *I renounce Satan and I cling to Jesus forever*, we could now dispense with religious practices. As ordained Christians, we possessed the necessary baggage for membership in the dominant community and the certitude that *there has to be something after death*.

Everyone knew how to distinguish between what was and was not done, between Good and Evil. Values could be read in others' eyes upon us. By their clothing, we could distinguish little girls from young girls, young girls from young ladies, young women from women, mothers from grandmothers, laborers from tradesmen and bureaucrats. Wealthy people said of shopgirls and typists who were too well dressed, "They wear their entire fortune on their backs."

Public or private, school was a place where immutable knowledge was imparted in silence and order, with respect for hierarchy and absolute submission, that is, to wear a smock, line up at the sound of the bell, stand when the headmistress or Mother Superior (but not a monitor) entered the room, acquire *regulation* notebooks, pens, and pencils, refrain from talking back when observations were made and from wearing trousers in the winter without a skirt over top. Only teachers were allowed to ask questions. If we did not understand a word or explanation, the fault was ours. We were proud, as of a privilege, to be bound by strict rules and confinement. The uniform required by private institutions was visible proof of their perfection.

The curriculum never changed, *Le médecin malgré lui* in the sixth grade, *Les fourberies de Scapin*, Racine's *Plaideurs*, and Victor Hugo's *Les pauvres gens* in the seventh, *Le Cid* in the eighth, etc. Nor did our textbooks, Malet-Isaac for history, Demangeon for geography, and Carpentier-Fialip for English. This body of knowledge was transferred to a minority whose intelligence and superiority was confirmed year after year, through *rosa rosam* and *Rome the only object of my resentment*, the Chasles relation and trigonometry while the majority continued doing mental arithmetic or problems involving trains, and singing *La Marseillaise* for the oral certificate. To pass the latter, or the *brevet*, was considered an event. The newspapers published the names of the students who had passed. Those who failed knew the weight of indignity at an early age. They were not *capable*. The speeches that praised education concealed its meager distribution.

If we met a former schoolmate who had enrolled in a commercial school or been sent to apprentice, it wouldn't occur to us to speak to her, although she'd shared our desk all the way to middle school. Nor would a lawyer's daughter with her fading ski-tan, proof of her superior social rank, so much as glance at us outside of school.

Work, effort, and willingness were the measures of behavior. On awards day, we were presented with books that extolled the heroism of aviation pioneers, generals, and colonizers— Mermoz, Leclerc de Lattre de Tassigny, Lyautey. Everyday courage was not forgotten either. One had to admire the father, "the adventurer of the modern world" (Péguy), "a humble life with boring and easy chores" (Verlaine), comment in writing on sayings by Georges Duhamel and Saint-Exupéry, and "the lesson in energy the heroes of Corneille teach us." We were asked to demonstrate how "love of family leads to love of country" and how "work keeps at bay three great evils: boredom, vice, and need" (Voltaire). We read *Vaillant* and *Âmes vaillantes.*[*]

To fortify youth in these ideals, toughen them physically, keep them safe from laziness and enfeebling pastimes (reading and films), make them into "decent young fellows" and "fine upstanding young ladies," families were advised to send their children to the Wolf Cubs, Pioneers, Girl Guides and Brownies, Crusaders and *Francas*. They would sit around a campfire in the evening, or march down a trail at dawn, wave a banner with martial fervor to the strains of "Akela's Trail," and attain an enchanted union of nature, order, and morality. Radiant faces looked to the future from the covers

---

[*] *Vaillant*, a young people's cartoon weekly with Communist roots, started in 1945. Now called *pif gadget*. *Âmes vaillantes*, founded in 1937, a Catholic *journal illustré* for young girls; a sister magazine to *Cœurs vaillants*, both associated with the eponymous Catholic youth movement.

of *La Vie Catholique* and *L'Humanité*. This wholesome youth, sons and daughters of France, followed in the footsteps of their *Résistant* elders, as President René Coty had proclaimed in a stirring speech of July 1954 at Place de la Gare, before a crowd of pupils grouped according to school, while white clouds scudded above in the storm-filled sky of a summer when the rain never stopped.

Somewhere below the ideal and the clear-eyed gazes, we knew, lay a shapeless oozing plain, riddled with other words, objects, images, and behaviors. Unwed mothers, the white slave trade, the movie posters from *Dear Caroline*, "rubbers," mysterious advertisements for "intimate hygiene, discretion guaranteed," the covers of *Health* magazine ("women are fertile only three days a month"), "love children," indecent assault, Janet Marshall strangled with her bra in the woods by the adulterer Robert Avril, the words "lesbian," "homosexual," "lust," and sins so abominable they couldn't even be brought to confession, miscarriage, nasty pastimes, books on the Index, *Tout ça parce qu'au bois de Chaville,* * free love, ad infinitum, a volume of unspeakable things only adults were supposed to know, the sum and substance of which were the genitals and their use. Sex was the root of all society's suspicions. People saw it everywhere, in everything: low necklines, tight skirts, red nail polish, black underwear, bikinis, the fraternizing of the sexes, the darkness of movie houses, public toilets, the muscles of Tarzan, women who smoked and crossed their legs, a girl's gesture of touching her hair in class, etc. It

---

* A song recounting a tryst in the woods at Chaville that results in the birth of a child, whose entire unfortunate life the singer foresees.

divided girls into a "right" and "wrong" kind. The moral rating posted on the church door for the weekly films was based on sex and sex alone.

But we outsmarted the surveillance and went to see *The Girl in the Bikini* and *Tempest in the Flesh* with Françoise Arnoul. We would have loved to resemble the movie heroines, possess the freedom to behave as they did. But between the films and books, on the one hand, and the dictates of society on the other, lay a vast zone of prohibition and moral judgment. To identify with anything we saw in the films or their heroines was forbidden.

In these conditions, we faced endless years of masturbation before making love permissibly in marriage. We had to live with our yearning for this pleasure that was considered the preserve of adults, which clamored for satisfaction at any cost, despite all attempts at prayer or diversion. Our lives were burdened with a secret that bracketed us with perverts, hysterics, and whores.

It was written in the Larousse:

Onanism: all means adopted to cause sexual enjoyment artificially. Onanism is often the cause of very serious accidents. Children must be supervised at the approach of puberty. Bromides, hydrotherapy, gymnastics, exercise, mountain cures, iron-based and arsenical medications, etc., will be alternately employed.

Whether under the bedclothes or in the lavatory, we masturbated before the eyes of all society.

Boys were proud to leave for their military service. We thought they looked handsome in their uniforms. On recruitment night, they made the rounds of the cafés to celebrate. It brought them glory to be recognized as real men. Before military service, they were still considered kids, devoid of status in the labor or marriage market. Afterwards, they could have a wife and children. The uniform they paraded through the neighborhood when they were on furlough lent them an aura of beauty and virtual sacrifice. The shadow of the victorious veterans, the GIs, hovered over them. The rough cloth of the jacket we brushed against as we stretched up to kiss them made tangible the absolute division between the worlds of men and women. When we looked at them we had a sense of heroism.

Beneath the surface of the things that never changed, last year's circus posters with the photo of Roger Lanzac, First Communion photos handed out to schoolmates, the *Club des chansonniers* on Radio Luxembourg, our days swelled with new desires. On Sunday afternoons, we crowded around the windows of the general electrics shop to watch television. Cafés invested in TV sets to lure clientele. Motocross trails wound up and down the hills, and we watched the deafening machines race all day. Commerce grew increasingly impatient and galvanized the daily routine of towns and cities with new watchwords such as "initiative" and "dynamism." The two-week trade fair became a fixture among the more traditional rites of spring, the funfair and the church bazaar. Loudspeakers bellowed sales pitches through the streets of the town center, interspersed with songs by Annie Cordy and Eddie Constantine. *Buy*, we were urged, to get a chance to win a Simca or a dining room suite. From the podium in front of the town hall, a local presenter entertained the crowd with the jokes of Roger Nicolas and Jean Richard, and rounded up candidates for quiz shows, *The Hook* or *Double or Nothing*, as on the radio. From a corner of the podium, the Queen of Commerce ruled from beneath her crown. The world of merchandise took advantage of the holiday to stake its claim. People said, "Gets you out of the house," and "It's a nice change, you don't want be an old stick-in-the-mud."

A diffuse joy spread among the young of the middle classes. They organized surprise parties—*surpats*—and invented a new vocabulary, *C'est cloche!*, *Formidable!*, *la vache*, adding *vachement* to every sentence, imitated the accent of la Marie-Chant*aaa*l,* played table soccer and called the parents' generation "old farts," snickered at Yvette Horner, Tino Rossi, and Bourvil. They sought models for their age, raved over Gilbert Bécaud and the broken chairs at his concert. They listened to Europe No. 1, which played only music, songs, and ads.

---

* A character invented in 1956, a *marie-chantal* or *la Marie-Chantal* is a prissy grande bourgeoise who is heedless of social realities other than her own.

In a black-and-white photo, two girls stand on a garden path, shoulder to shoulder, arms folded behind their backs. Behind them, flowering shrubs and a high brick wall, above them, sky with big white clouds. On the back: *July 1955, St. Michel Convent School grounds*.

The taller girl, on the left, is blonde with short tousled hair, a light-colored dress, and ankle socks. Her face is in shadow. The one on the right is brunette with short curly hair, a high forehead, and glasses. A shaft of light lies across her rounded face. She wears a dark short-sleeved sweater and a polka-dot skirt. Both wear ballerina flats, the brunette barefoot in hers. They have removed their school smocks for the photo.

Even if we don't recognize the brunette as the girl in pigtails from the photo on the beach (she could just as easily have become the blonde), it was she, and not the blonde, who was that consciousness, captured inside that body, with a unique memory thanks to which we are able to confirm that the curly hair is the result of a perm, a May ritual since the year of her Holy Communion, the skirt cut from a dress worn the previous summer and grown too tight, the sweater knit by a neighbor. And it is with the perceptions and sensations received by the spectacled fourteen-and-a-half-year-old brunette that this writing is able to retrieve something slipping through the 1950s, capture the reflection that collective history projects upon the screen of individual memory.

Apart from the ballerina flats, nothing in the appearance of this teenage girl reflects what was "all the rage" that year or what was in the fashion magazines and the big-city stores, long plaid midi-skirts, black sweaters, and chunky lockets, ponytails and bangs like Audrey Hepburn's in *Roman Holiday*. The photo could easily date from the late forties or early sixties. For those born later it is simply old, and belongs to the prehistory of self, where all lives that precede one's own are leveled and disappear. Yet the beam that lights one side of the girl's face and the sweater, between the breasts, was for her a sensation of heat from the June sun of a year that no historian, or anyone else who lived at the time, could mistake for any other but 1955.

Maybe she does not perceive the gap that separates her from other girls in her class, the ones with whom it would be unimaginable to have her picture taken. The gap between them can be seen in their respective diversions, how they spend their time outside of school, and their general way of life, which set her apart as much from the well-off girls as from those employed in offices and factories. Or perhaps she has a good idea of the gap but doesn't give it a thought.

She has never been to Paris, one hundred and forty kilometers away, or to a *surpat*. She doesn't have a record player. While doing homework, she listens to songs on the radio, copies the lyrics into a notebook, and carries them inside her head for days while walking or sitting in class, *toi qui disais qui disais que tu l'aimais, tu l'aimais, tu l'aimais qu'as-tu fait de ton amour pour qu'il pleure sous la pluie.*

She doesn't talk to boys, but thinks about them all the time. She'd like to be allowed to wear lipstick, stockings, and high heels. Ankle socks are a disgrace, she takes them off as soon as she leaves the house to show that she belongs to the *jeune fille* category and can be followed in the street. To this end, on Sunday mornings after Mass, she "hangs out" in town with two or three friends who share her "humble background," always careful not to break the strict maternal law of the witching hour—*that time* ("When I give you a time, I mean *that time*, and not a minute later"). She compensates for the curfew by reading the serial novels, *Les gens de Mogador, Afin que nul ne meure, My Cousin Rachel, La citadelle*. She constantly steps out of herself and into stories, imagined meetings that end in orgasms under the sheets at night. She imagines herself as a whore, yearns after the blonde in the photo and the girls in the grade ahead, who bring her back to her smeared and sticky body. She would like to be them.

She has seen *La strada, The Unfrocked One, The Proud and the Beautiful, The Rains of Ranchipur, La belle de Cadix*. The number of films she wants to see that are forbidden, *Children of Love, The Game of Love, The Companions of the Night*, etc., outnumber the ones that are allowed.

(One possible summary of the life of a provincial teen: going up to town, daydreaming, bringing oneself to orgasm and waiting.)

What knowledge of the world does her mind contain, outside of what she's learned in school so far, in eighth grade? What does she know of the events and news items that will make people say "I remember that!" when a phrase heard by chance calls them to mind?

—the great train strike of the summer of '53
—the fall of Dien Bien Phu
—Stalin's death announced on the radio, one cold morning in March, just before children left for school

—primary school pupils lining up at the canteen to drink the glass of milk from Mendès France*

—the blanket of squares knitted by all the students and sent to Abbé Pierre, whose beard gives them fodder for dirty jokes

—smallpox vaccinations at the town hall for the entire town because several people had died of it in Vannes

—the floods in Holland

There is probably nothing in her thoughts about the most recent deaths from an ambush in Algeria, the latest episode in the troubles, which started on All Saints' Day in 1954, but she will only know this later. She will see herself again that day in her room, sitting next to the window with her feet on the bed. She watched guests emerge one after the other from a house across the road to urinate behind the blind wall in the garden. And so she will never forget the date of the insurrection in Algeria, nor that All Saints' afternoon, of which she will retain one clear image, a kind of pure fact: a young woman squatting over the grass, as if to lay an egg, and standing again, pushing her skirts down.

To this storehouse of illegitimate memory she consigns things too unthinkable, shameful, or crazy to put into words:

—a brown stain on a sheet of her mother's that had once belonged to her grandmother, dead for three years—an indelible spot that violently attracts and repels her, as if it were alive

—the scene between her parents on the Sunday before her sixth-grade entrance exam, when her father tried to kill her mother, dragging her to the cellar next to the block where they kept the sickle planted

---

* In 1954, Prime Minister Pierre Mendès France initiated a milk-drinking campaign to combat malnutrition among schoolchildren and alcoholism in the general population.

—the memory that comes to her every day on the way to school as she passes an embankment where, two years earlier, on a Sunday in January, she saw a little girl in a short coat gleefully sinking her foot into the water-gorged clay. The footprint was there the next day and remained for months.

The summer holidays will be a long stretch of boredom and minuscule activities conceived to fill the days:
—listening to the arrival of each stage of the Tour de France; pasting the winner's photo into a special album
—watching cars go by and writing down the department numbers from the license plates
—in the regional newspaper, reading the summaries of films she will not see and books she will not read
—embroidering a napkin ring
—squeezing blackheads without applying Eau Précieuse or lemon slices
—going up to town to buy shampoo and a *Petit classique Larousse*, and then, eyes downcast, passing the café where the boys are playing pinball

The future is too immense for her to imagine. It will happen, that's all.

When she hears the little pre-school girls in the playground singing *Cueillons la rose sans la laisser flétrir*, it seems to her a very long time since she was a child.

In the mid-1950s, at family meals, teenagers remained at the table. They listened but did not speak, smiled politely at the jokes that were not funny, the approving comments whose object was their physical development, the salty innuendos designed to make them blush, and answered only the cautious questions about their schoolwork. They did not feel ready to enter fully and legitimately into general conversation, though the wine, liqueurs, and blonde cigarettes they were allowed at dessert marked a first induction into the adult circle. They let themselves be permeated by the kindness of the festive group, whose social judgment, usually harsh, had abated and turned into gentle amenity. The mortal enemies of the year before, reconciled, passed each other the mayonnaise bowl. We were a little bored, but not so much that we'd have preferred to be sitting in the next day's math class.

Comments were made on each course as it was consumed, summoning memories of the same dish eaten in other circumstances and advice on the best way to prepare it, followed by debate on flying saucers—were they real?—and who would be the first to reach the moon, the Americans or the Russians. They discussed Sputnik, Abbé Pierre's emergency settlements, and the high cost of living. Then the war was back on the table. They recalled the exodus, bombardments, and postwar restrictions, zoot suits and golf pants. We listened to the romance of our birth and early childhood with an indefinable nostalgia, the same we felt when passionately reciting *Rappelle-toi, Barbara*, whose lyrics we'd copied into a secret notebook of poems. But we sensed distance in the voices. Something had died with the grandparents, who had seen both wars, the growing of children, the full reconstruction of cities, progress, and furniture on the installment plan. The Occupation and rural childhoods with all their privations merged into a single bygone era. People were so thoroughly convinced that life was better now.

There was no more talk of Indochina, so distant and exotic—"two bags of rice at either end of a bamboo pole," according to the geography book—and lost without great regret at Dien Bien Phu. Only diehards had fought in that battle, the *engagé* volunteers who lacked other occupations. That conflict had never been part of anyone's present life. Nor did the company wish to darken the atmosphere by bringing up Algeria. No one knew how the troubles there had started, but they all agreed, as did we, who'd studied it for the *brevet* exam, that Algeria, with its three *départements*, was French, like much of Africa, where our territories covered half the continent in the atlas. Of course, someone had to suppress the rebellion, clean up the "nests of fellaghas," the cutthroats whose treacherous shadows one saw in the dark face of *sidi-my-goood-fréennde* the peddler (though he seemed a nice enough fellow) who sold bedside rugs off his back. Added to the derision to which the Arabs and their language were ritually subjected, *habana la moukère mets ton nez dans le cafetière tu verras si c'est chaud*, was a certainty of their essential savagery. So it was only right that new and recalled conscripts be sent there to restore order, although everyone agreed it was unfortunate for parents to lose a twenty-year-old son, about to be married, whose photo appeared in the regional newspaper with the caption "Killed in an ambush." These were individual tragedies, a death here, a death there. No enemy, no soldiers, no battle. No feeling of war. The next one would come from the East with

Russian tanks, as in Budapest, to destroy the free world. There'd be no point in taking to the roads as one had done in 1940. With the atomic bomb, no one stood a chance. As it was, the Suez Canal affair had been a very close call.

No one talked about concentration camps, except incidentally, to say that someone had lost his or her parents at Buchenwald. Sorrowful silence would follow. It had entered the realm of private misfortune.

The patriotic songs from after the Liberation were no longer brought out at dessert. The parents sang Dalida's *Parlez-moi d'amour*, the older young people *Mexico,* and the children *My Granny Was a Cowboy*. We'd have been too ashamed to sing *Etoile des neiges* as before. When they begged us for a tune, we claimed not to know any in full. We were sure that Brassens and Brel would fall like lead balloons on the end-of-meal beatitude. We felt that what was needed were the songs sanctified by other meals and tears dabbed away with the corners of napkins. We were fiercely opposed to *disclosing* musical tastes they wouldn't understand. The only English words the others knew were *fuck you*, learned at the time of the Liberation. They were unaware that the Platters and Bill Haley even existed.

But the next day, in the silence of the study hall, we knew from our feeling of emptiness that the previous day, much as we had pushed it away, believing ourselves bored and alienated, had truly been a holiday.

The few young people lucky enough to remain in school were drawn into the infinitely slow time of study—the regular chiming of class bells, the return of quarterly compositions, the endless explanations of *Cinna* and *Iphigenia*, the translation of the *Pro Milone*—and felt as if nothing ever happened. We scribbled down writers' reflections on life, discovered the joys of describing ourselves to ourselves with shimmering turns of phrase, *existence is to drink oneself without thirst*. We were overcome by nausea and a feeling of the absurd. The sticky body of adolescence met the *être en trop* of existentialism. On our binders we pasted photos of Brigitte Bardot in *And God Created Woman*, and carved James Dean's initials into our desks. We copied out the poems of Prévert, the songs of Brassens, *Je suis un voyou* and *La première fille*, which were banned from the radio. On the sly, we read *Bonjour Tristesse* and *Three Essays on the Theory of Sexuality*. The sphere of desires and prohibitions was becoming immense. We glimpsed the possibility of a world without sin. Adults suspected us of being *corrupted* by modern writers and of *having no respect for anything*.

For now, our most stubborn desire was to possess a record player and a few LPs, expensive objects we could enjoy alone, endlessly, ad nauseam, or with others, those considered the most progressive among all the tribes of youth, the affluent high school girls who wore duffel coats, called their parents "the oldsters," and said *ciao* instead of goodbye.

We could not get our fill of jazz, Negro spirituals, and rock 'n' roll. Everything sung in English was suffused with mysterious beauty. *Dream, love, heart,* words of great purity and no practical use, conveyed the sense of a world-beyond. In the privacy of our rooms, we engaged in solitary orgies of playing the same disc over and over. It was like a drug that blew the mind away, smashed the body, and opened a whole new world of love and violence, inseparable from *surboums,* those unbridled parties we interminably longed to attend. Elvis Presley, Bill Haley, Armstrong and the Platters embodied modernity, the future. They sang for us alone, for the young, leaving behind the antiquated tastes of parents, the ignorance of country bumpkins, *Le Pays du sourire,* André Claveau and Line Renaud. We felt ourselves part of a circle of the enlightened. Still, Piaf's *Les Amants d'un jour* gave us goosebumps.

Again we were back in the silence of vacation, the distinct, separate sounds of the provinces—the footsteps of a woman on her way to do her shopping, a car swishing by, the pounding from a welding shop. We drained the hours with tiny goals, and activities we made to last as long as possible. We filed last year's homework, tidied a closet, read a novel, trying not to finish too quickly. We gazed at ourselves in the mirror and willed our hair to grow long enough for a ponytail. We kept an eye out for the unlikely arrival of a friend. At supper it was like pulling teeth to get us to speak. We didn't finish our food and were reproached, "If you'd gone hungry during the war, you wouldn't be so fussy." In opposition to the desires that made us restless, we were served the wisdom of limits: "You ask too much of life."

Girls and boys hung around in separate packs, crossing paths on Sunday after Mass or at the movies. Glances were exchanged and then inevitably they spoke. The boys mimicked teachers, reeled off puns and spoonerisms, called each other fairies, cut each other off—"You don't have to tell us the story of your life," "Please shut your mouth when you're talking to me," "You seem a little gassy, go home and boil an egg." They delighted in talking so quietly that we didn't understand and then yelling, "Masturbation makes you deaf!" They pretended to cover their eyes before the sight of a boy's swollen gums and cried: "We saw enough horrors in the war!" They assumed the right to say whatever came to mind. They were custodians of the word and of humor. They unleashed a flood of dirty stories and gravely intoned the *De Profundis Morpionibus.** The girls replied with distant smiles. They didn't necessarily find them funny, but knew that all the swirling and hovering was a show the boys put on for their benefit, and the girls were rightly proud. The boys supplied words and expressions that would make the girls seem advanced in the eyes of other girls, as when they said *Time to hit the hay* and *Nice threads!* But anxiously they wondered what they would say if ever they were alone with a boy. They needed the whole group's curious solicitude for support, every step of the way until the first date.

---

* A mock-serious libertine ballad sung to the tune of a funeral march with words by Théophile Gautier (1864), the subject of which is pubic lice and the battle to overcome them.

The distance that separates past from present can be measured, perhaps, by the light that spills across the ground between shadows, slips over faces, outlines the folds of a dress—by the twilight clarity of a black-and-white photo, no matter what time it is taken.

In this photo, a tall girl blinks against the sun. Her hair is dark, shoulder-length and straight, her face smooth and full. She stands at an oblique angle, one hip slightly outthrust to emphasize the swell of the thighs in the pencil skirt, while making them look slimmer. The light grazes her right cheekbone and accentuates her chest, which presses out from under the sweater. A white Peter Pan collar is folded over the neck of the sweater. One arm is hidden while the other hangs at her side, the sleeve rolled up above a wristwatch and a broad hand. The contrast with the photo from the school garden is striking. Other than the cheekbones and the shape of the breasts, now more developed, there is nothing to remind us of the girl with glasses of two years ago. She poses in a courtyard that gives onto the street, in front of a low shed with a patchily mended door, the kind one sees in the country and close suburbs. In the background, the trunks of three trees planted on a high embankment stand out against the sky. On the back of the photo: *1957, Yvetot.*

At the precise moment when she smiles, she is probably thinking only of herself, of this photo of herself gazing at the new girl she feels herself becoming:

—when, in the tiny island of her bedroom, she listens to Sidney Béchet, Édith Piaf, and the 33 rpms ordered from the Concert Hall Record Club

—when she copies down sentences that tell one how to live, which have the undeniable weight of truth because they come from books: *There is no real happiness except that which we are aware of while we are feeling it*

Now she is aware of her social standing. Her family doesn't have a Frigidaire or a bathroom, the lavatories are at the back of the yard and she still hasn't been to Paris. She is lower down on the social scale than her schoolmates. She hopes they won't notice, or that if they do, she'll be forgiven because she is "fun," "a good sport," calls a person's home their "pad," and says, "That gives me the screaming meemies."

All her energy is focused on "having a certain something." Her major worry remains her glasses for myopia. They make her eyes look smaller and give her an "egghead" look, but if she takes them off she doesn't recognize anyone on the street.

When she imagines herself in the more distant future, after the *bac*,* she models her body and her general look on photos from women's magazines. She is thin with long billowing hair, like Marina Vlady in *The Blonde Witch*, and has become a teacher somewhere, perhaps in the country, free and independent. She has her own car, the ultimate sign of emancipation—a 2CV or 4CV. Across this image lies the shadow of a man, a stranger she'll meet, as in the Mouloudji song *Un jour tu verras*. Or they'll run into each other's arms, like Michèle Morgan and Gérard Philipe at the end of *Les orgueilleux*. She knows she

* *Bac*, or *baccalauréat*, a diploma passed at the end of secondary school, a prerequisite for university. Until 1963, it included two parts; the second *bac* exam was written a year after the first, and was equivalent to a B.A. degree.

must "save herself for him" and considers her knowledge of solitary pleasure an offense against Great Love. Though she's written down the days when there is no risk of pregnancy, according to the Ogino* method, she is all emotion. Sex and love are worlds apart.

Her life beyond the *bac* is a stairway rising into the mist.

With the abbreviated memory one needs at sixteen simply to act and exist, she sees her childhood as a sort of silent film in color. Images of tanks and rubble appear and blur with others of old people who have died, hand-made Mother's Day cards, the *Bécassine* albums, the First Communion retreat, games of sixes played against a wall. Nor does she care to remember the more recent years, all awkwardness and shame—the time she dressed up as a music-hall dancer, the curly permanent, ankle socks.

From 1957, she will remember (but does not yet know it):
—the Sunday afternoon in the bar of the beach casino in Fécamp where, fascinated, she watched a couple dance to slow blues on the deserted dance floor, their bodies pressed against each other. The woman was willowy and blonde, and wore a white dress with "accordion" pleats. Her parents, whom she'd dragged into the bar against their will, wondered if they had enough money to pay for the drinks
—the icy lavatories in the schoolyard, where she'd had to retreat one February day in the middle of math class with an attack

---

* A method proposed by the Japanese obstetrician Dr. Ogino in the 1920s to calculate the optimum period for conception. Later, it was popularized as a method of birth control (a.k.a. the rhythm method).

of gastroenteritis. Her thighs marbled with cold, her insides twisting in pain, she thought of Roquentin in the public garden and said to herself *The sky is empty and God does not answer.* She has no name for that feeling of utter abandonment, nor the feeling that comes over her on fair days, when she stands in the courtyard from the photo, and the voice of the loudspeaker booms from behind the trees, and the music and commercials run together in an unintelligible blur. It is as if she were standing outside the fête, separated from some earlier thing.

No doubt the information she receives about world events is transformed into sensations, feelings, and images with no trace of the ideologies that initially provoked them. And so what she sees is:

—Europe bisected by a great iron wall, sunshine and color to the west, and to the east darkness, cold, snow, and Soviet tanks that one day will cross the French border, invade Paris as they had Budapest; the names Imre Nagy and Kadar obsess her, and from time to time she rolls the syllables on her tongue

—in Algeria of the scorched and blood-soaked earth, gutted by ambushes, small men in swirling burnooses flutter, as in *The Taking of the Smalah of Abd-el-Kader,* a painting she remembers from her ninth-grade history book, depicting the conquest of Algeria in 1830

—the dead soldiers in the Aurès Mountains of Algeria resemble Rimbaud's *Sleeper in the Valley*; as in the poem, they lie in the sand where *the light falls like rain* with *two red holes in their right side*

These representations, which probably convey assent to the repression of the rebels, are undermined by a photo in the local paper of stylish French youths, deep in discussion at the door of a high school in Bab el-Oued, as if to say the cause for which twenty-year-old soldiers die is not so easy to justify.

None of this appears in the diary she has started to keep, in which she describes her boredom and the long wait for love in high-flown, sentimental prose. She mentions that she has to write an essay on *Polyeucte* but prefers the novels of Françoise Sagan, "which, though fundamentally immoral, have the ring of truth."

More than ever, people relied upon the acquisition of things to build better lives. According to their means, they exchanged the coal-fueled stove for a gas cooker, the oilcloth-covered wooden table for Formica-topped, the 4CV for a Dauphine. The old-fashioned safety razor and cast-iron steam iron were replaced with electrical equivalents, metal utensils with plastic. The most enviable and expensive object was the automobile, synonymous with freedom, a total mastery of space and, in a certain way, the world. To learn to drive and get your license was considered a victory, hailed by friends and family as when you passed the *brevet* at the end of ninth grade.

People enrolled in correspondence courses to learn drawing, English, secretarial skills, or jujitsu. *These days we need to know more*, they said. A new profusion of *F* stickers on license plates proved they no longer feared vacationing abroad without speaking the language. On Sundays the beaches were crowded with bikini-clad bodies, bared to the sun and the gaze of all. It was less and less "done" to remain sitting on the beach, or to gather one's skirts and wade in up to the ankles. People said of the shy or of anyone who didn't yield to the joys of the group, "They've got hang-ups." It was the dawning of the "society of leisure."

But they grew heated over politics and lost their tempers. Prime ministers were shown the door every two months, the young tirelessly sent off to be killed in ambushes. People wanted peace in Algeria but not a second Dien Bien Phu. They voted for Poujade. "Where are we going?" they repeated. The coup d'état of May 13 in Algiers put them into a state of catastrophe. They stockpiled kilos of sugar, liters of oil in preparation for civil war. None but General de Gaulle, they believed, could save Algeria and France. They were relieved when the savior of 1940 magnanimously agreed to return and take the country in hand, as if they felt protected by the long shadow of the man whose great height, the object of their constant jokes, was visible proof of his superhuman status.

We who remembered the gaunt face from the posters in the ruined town, the kepi and the little prewar mustache, we who had not heard the appeal of June 18, 1940, were startled and disappointed to hear the old-man's quaver in the voice, see the jowly cheeks and bushy eyebrows that made one think of a country notary run to fat. The personage summoned from Colombey made it grotesquely clear how much time had passed since we were children. We resented him for so rapidly thwarting, while we were reviewing sines and cosines and *Lagarde et Michard*,* what had seemed to us the start of a revolution.

---

* Six-volume textbook series on French literature from the Middle Ages to the twentieth century, first published in 1948 and used in schools for decades.

"To get your two *bacs*"—the first at the end of the eleventh grade, the second the year after—was an incontestable sign of intellectual superiority, a guarantee of future social success. For most of those around us, the exams and competitions that we would later sit were less important than the *bac*. They said it was "nice to have got even this far."

To the rousing theme from *The Bridge On the River Kwai*, we set out for what we felt would be the summer of our lives. The passing of the *bac* granted us social existence. We had proved *not unworthy* of the adults' faith in us. Parents arranged to make the rounds of family and friends to break the glorious news. But then, at first imperceptibly, that July began to resemble the one of the year before with convoluted schedules of LP listening, reading, and scribbling the first lines of poems. Our euphoria waned. To restore the value of our success, we needed reminders of how the summer would have been had we failed. The true reward for passing the *bac* would have been a love affair, like the one in *Marianne of My Youth*. In the meantime, we flirted, secretly met with a boy who went a little lower each time, and whom we'd have to leave soon, for we were not about to lose our virginity to a boy our girlfriends referred to as Lobster Face.

Space opened up at last that summer, or maybe it was another. The wealthiest students left with their parents for England or the French Riviera. Others went to summer camps to work as counselors, enjoy a change of air, see more of France, and pay for the next year's schoolbooks. They trekked down country roads singing *Pirouette cacahouète* with a dozen twittering little boys or clingy little girls, with a bag of snacks and the snake bite kit slung over their shoulder. They received their first wages and a social security number, proud of their responsibilities as interim purveyors of the secular republican ideal, joyously implemented through its "active education methods." They supervised the Lion Cubs at the sinks as they washed and brushed their teeth, all in a row in their underpants. They presided at chaotic tables where the arrival of rice pudding raised howls of enthusiasm, and firmly believed they were helping to build a model of order that was just, harmonious, and good. All in all, it was a glorious and grueling holiday, sure to never be forgotten, especially not the heady new mingling of the sexes, far from parental eyes at last, and how, wearing jeans, Gauloise in hand, we took the stairs two at a time down to a cellar and the music of a *surboum*. A feeling of absolute, precarious youth washed over us, as if we were fated to die at the end of the holidays like the girl in *She Danced Only One Summer*. Borne on this tide of emotion, we moved from a slow dance to a cot, or the beach, with a man's sex (only seen in photos, and even then . . .) and semen in our mouth, having recalled the Ogino calendar just in time and refused to open our thighs. Day broke, pallid and meaningless. Over the top of the phrases we'd wanted to forget as soon as we'd heard them, *put my cock in your mouth, suck me*, we had to write the words of a love song instead, *that morning was yesterday, only yesterday and already far away*, to make it beautiful, construct a romantic fiction about "the first time," and shroud in melancholy the memory of a failed deflowering. And if that didn't work, we'd buy éclairs and sweets—whipped cream and sugar to drown our sorrows, or anorexia to purge them. But one thing was certain: it would never again be possible to remember how the world had been before the night we lay with a naked body pressed to ours.

For girls, shame lay in wait at every turn. The verdict of *too* loomed large over their clothing and makeup: too short, long, low-cut, tight, flashy, etc. The height of their heels, whom they saw, what time they went out and came in, the crotch of their underwear, month after month, were subject to all-pervasive surveillance by society. For those obliged to leave the family fold, society provided the Young Ladies' Residence, separate from the boys' dorm, to protect them from men and vice. Nothing, not intelligence, education, or beauty mattered as much as a girl's sexual reputation, that is, her value on the marriage market, which mothers scrupulously monitored as their mothers had done before them. "If you have sex before marriage, no one will want you," they said, the subtext of which was no one except a market reject of the male variety, an invalid, a madman, or worse, a divorcé. The unwed mother lost her entire worth and had nothing to hope for, except perhaps a man who would sacrifice himself and take her in, along with the fruit of her sin.

Until marriage, love stories were played out before the eyes and judgments of others.

Still one flirted and went farther each time, resorting to practices unnamed except in the medical literature, fellatio, cunnilingus, and sometimes sodomy. Boys made fun of rubbers and rejected the coitus interruptus practiced by their fathers. We dreamed of contraceptive pills, sold in Germany, so people claimed. On Saturdays, girls in white veils lined up to be married, giving birth six months later to robust "premature" babies. Between the freedom of Bardot, the taunting of boys who claimed that virginity was bad for the health, and the dictates of Church and parents, we were left with no choices at all. No one asked how long abortion and living together outside of marriage would remain outlawed. Signs of collective change cannot be perceived in the specific features of lives, except perhaps in the disgust and fatigue that led thousands of individuals at once to think, in exasperation, "So that's how it is—nothing will ever change."

In the black-and-white group photo, inserted in an embossed folder, twenty-six girls stand in three tiered rows in a courtyard, under the leaves of a chestnut tree, against a façade whose small-paned windows could be those of a convent, a school, or a hospital. All the girls wear pale smocks that give them the look of a nursing corps.

Below the photo, written by hand: *Lycée Jeanne-d'Arc— Rouen—Philosophy section, Class of 1958–1959.* The names have not been inscribed, as if when the class president delivered the photos, it had been unthinkable that any could be forgotten. Certainly, none of the girls could have imagined herself forty years later, an elderly woman looking at faces once so familiar and seeing only a triple row of ghosts with bright fixed gazes.

The girls in the front row sit on tube chairs, hands folded in their laps, legs straight and pressed together or tucked under the chair. Only one has her legs crossed. The girls in the second row, who stand on the ground, and the ones in the third row, who stand on a bench, are visible from the hips up. Only six have their hands in their pockets, a sign of poor upbringing at the time, which suggests that the lycée is mainly attended by daughters of the bourgeoisie. All but four gaze at the lens, faintly smiling. What the four are looking at—the photographer, a wall, other students?—is lost to history.

She is in the second row, third from the left. It is difficult to see in her the girl with the provocative pose from the previous photo, taken scarcely two years earlier. She wears glasses again, and a ponytail from which a lock of hair escapes at the neck. Frizzy bangs do nothing to soften her serious demeanor. Her face bears no sign of the events of the summer before, the boy's invasion of her being, her semi-defloration evinced by the bloodstained underwear hidden between some books in her cupboard. No sign, either, of her actions and movements after the event: walking the streets after school in hopes of seeing him; returning to the young ladies' residence and weeping. Spending hours on an essay topic and understanding nothing. Playing *Only You* over and over when she returns to her parents' home on Saturdays, stuffing herself with bread, biscuits, and chocolate.

No sign of the heaviness of existence she must tear herself away from to master the language of philosophy, serve the injunction of essence and the categorical imperative, subjugate the body, repress the desire for food and the obsession with the monthly blood that no longer flows. Reflect on the real so it will cease to be real, become an abstract thing—intangible, a product of intelligence. A few weeks later, she will stop eating, buy Néo-Antigrès fat-burning pills, and be reduced to pure consciousness. After class, when she walks up boulevard du Marne, past the funfair booths, the howl of the music follows her like calamity.

Not all of the twenty-six students in the photo talk to each other. Each girl speaks to only ten or twelve others, ignores the rest and is ignored by them. All know by instinct what to do when they pass each other on the street near the lycée: whether to wait, or smile but nothing more, or simply not see each other. But from metaphysics hour to gym class, all the voices that answer "present" in the roll call, all the physical features and clothing are inscribed in each girl's conscious-ness. Every student has inside her a sample of each of the other twenty-five. In this class, a total of twenty-six view-points are in constant circulation, freighted with judgments and feelings. No more than any of her classmates can the girl say how others see her. More than anything she wants not to be seen. She wants to be one of the ignored, good stu-dents, without luster or repartee. She is unwilling to say her parents run a café-épicerie, ashamed that she is haunted by food, that her period has stopped, that she doesn't know the meaning of *hypokhâgne*,* and wears a jacket of imitation suede

---

* *Hypokhâgne*: prepatory class for advanced studies in arts and literature at the *École normale supérieure*, followed by the *Khâgne*. Both are informal, pseudo-Greek expressions, based on the word *cagneux*, meaning "knock-kneed."

instead of real. She feels very lonely. She reads *Dusty Answer* by Rosamond Lehmann and everything she can in the *Modern Poets* series, Supervielle, Milosz, Apollinaire, *Do I know, my love, if you still love me?*

Of all the ways in which self-knowledge may be fostered, perhaps one of the greatest is a person's ability to discern how they view the past, at every time of life and every age; if that is so, what kind of memory can be ascribed to this girl in the second row? Maybe she has no memory except that of the previous summer, almost bereft of images—the incorporation of a missing body, a man's. Two future goals coexist inside her: (1) to be thin and blonde, (2) to be free, autonomous, and useful to the world. She dreams of herself as Mylène Demongeot and Simone de Beauvoir.

Though reserve soldiers continued to leave for Algeria, it was a time of hope and striving, of grand designs for land, sea, and sky; a time of great words and great losses, too, those of Gérard Philipe and Camus. There would be the SS *France*, the Caravelle jetliner, and the Concorde, school until sixteen, centers of arts and culture, the Common Market, and, sooner or later, peace in Algeria. There were new francs, scoubidou bracelets, flavored yogurt, milk in pyramid-shaped cartons, transistor radios. For the first time one could listen to music anywhere, whether one was lying on the beach with the radio next to one's head, or walking down the street. The joy of the transistor was of an unknown species. One could be alone but not alone, and have at one's command the noise and diversity of the world.

And the young continued to arrive in ever-increasing numbers, and teachers were in short supply. One needed only be eighteen and have passed the *bac* to be sent to a preparatory class and guide it through *Rémi and Colette*. We were provided with sources of diversion, the Hula-Hoop and wholesome reading for young adults, but were not allowed to do anything that mattered, neither vote nor make love, or even state an opinion. To have the right to be heard, one first had to prove one's ability to blend in with the dominant social model, "go into" teaching, join La Poste or SNCF rail, Michelin, or Gillette, enter the insurance sector, "earn a living." The future was a series of experiences to carry forward, military service for twenty-four months, work, marriage, and children. We were expected to perpetuate tradition as a matter of course. In the face of this compulsory future, we vaguely yearned to stay young for a long, long time. Discourse and institutions had not caught up to our desires, but for us the gulf between society's "sayable" and our unsayable seemed normal and irremediable. It was something we couldn't think but only feel, deep inside, alone watching *Breathless*.

People had had more than enough of Algeria, OAS bombs on Paris windowsills, the Petit-Clamart attack. Enough of waking up to the news of a coup by unknown generals that disrupted the march toward peace and "self-determination." They had got used to the ideas of independence and the legitimacy of the FLN, learned the names of its leaders, Ben Bella and Ferhat Abbas. Their desire for happiness and tranquillity tallied with the introduction of a principle of justice: decolonization, previously unthinkable. However, they still exhibited as much fear as ever, or at best indifference, in relation to "the Arabs," whom they avoided and ignored. They could not be reconciled to sharing streets with individuals whose brothers had murdered Frenchmen across the Mediterranean. And the immigrant worker, when he passed a French man or woman on the street, knew more quickly and clearly than they that he wore the face of the enemy. That "Arabs" lived in slums, labored on assembly lines or at the bottom of pits, their October demonstration outlawed, then suppressed with the most extreme violence, and maybe even (that is, had we been aware of it) that a hundred had been thrown into the Seine, seemed to be in the nature of things. (Later, when we learned what had happened on October 17, 1961, we were unable to say what we had *known* at the time, recalling nothing except balmy weather and the imminent return to university. We felt the unease of *not having known*, though the State and the press had done everything to keep us in the dark, as if there were no making up for past ignorance and silence. And try as we might, we would see no resemblance between October's heinous attack on Algerians by Gaullist police and the attack on anti-OAS militants the following February. The nine dead crushed against the railings of the Charonne Métro station bore no comparison with the uncounted dead of the Seine.)

Nobody asked whether the Évian Accords were a victory or a defeat. They brought relief and the beginning of forgetting. We did not concern ourselves with what would happen next for the Pieds-Noirs and the Harkis in Algeria, or the Algerians in France. We hoped to go to Spain the following summer—a real bargain, according to everyone who'd been there.

People were accustomed to violence and separation in the world. East/West, Khrushchev the muzhik/Kennedy the leading man, Peppone/Don Camillo, JEC/UEC, *L'Humanité/L'Aurore*, Franco/Tito, Cathos/Commies. Under cover from the Cold War, they felt calm. Outside of union speeches with their codified violence, they did not complain, having made up their minds to be kept by the State, listen to Jean Nocher moralize on the radio each night, and not see the strikes amount to anything. When they voted yes in the October referendum, it was less from a desire to elect the president of the Republic through universal suffrage than from a secret wish to keep de Gaulle president for life, if not until the end of time.

Meanwhile, we studied for our second *bac* while listening to the transistor. We went to see *Cléo from 5 to 7*, *Last Year at Marienbad*, Bergman, Buñuel and Italian films. We loved Léo Ferré, Barbara, Jean Ferrat, Leny Escudero, and Claude Nougaro. We read *Hara-Kiri*. We felt nothing in common with the yé-yés, who said *Hitler, never heard of him*, and their idols, who were even younger than we: girls with pigtails and songs for the schoolyard; a boy who bellowed and writhed on the floor of the stage. We had the feeling they'd never catch up to us. Next to them, we were old. Perhaps we too would die under de Gaulle.

But we were not adults. Sexual life remained clandestine and rudimentary, haunted by the specter of "an accident." No one was supposed to have a sex life before marriage. Boys believed their lewd innuendos displayed advanced erotic science, but all they knew how to do was ejaculate on an area of the girl's body to which she directed him, for the sake of caution. No one knew for sure whether or not they were still virgins. Sexuality was a poorly resolved matter on which girls held forth for hours in residence rooms no boy was allowed to enter. They did their reading, pored through Kinsey to convince themselves of the legitimacy of pleasure. They had inherited their mothers' shame about sex. There were still men's words and women's words. Girls did not say "come" or "cock," or anything at all. They recoiled from naming the organs except to say "vagina" or "penis" in a special toneless voice. The boldest of them stole out to see a counselor at Family Planning, an underground organization, and were prescribed rubber diaphragms that they struggled to insert.

They had no idea that the boys they attended lectures with were frightened of their bodies, that if they answered their most innocent questions with monosyllables, it was not from contempt but from fear of the inherent complications of their snap-jaw bellies. All things considered, they preferred to quietly beat off at night.

Having failed to panic in time, somewhere in a pinewood or on the sands of Costa Brava, one saw Time stand still before a pair of underpants whose crotch had remained spotless for days. "It" had to be got rid of, one way or another. Rich girls went to Switzerland, others to the kitchen of an unspecialized, unknown woman with a probe boiled in a stewpot. The fact of having read Simone de Beauvoir was of no use except to confirm the misfortune of having a womb. So, like sick people, three weeks out of four girls took their temperatures to calculate the risks, and lived in two different times. One was everybody's time, with class presentations and holidays; the other, fickle and treacherous, liable to stop at any moment, was the deadly time ruled by their blood.

In lecture halls, professors in neckties explained writers' works by way of their biographies. They said "Monsieur" André Malraux and "Madame" Yourcenar, out of respect for the living persons, and had us study dead authors only. We didn't dare quote Freud, fearing sarcasm and bad marks. We barely even mentioned Bachelard and *Studies in Human Time* by Georges Poulet, believed we showed great independence of mind by declaring at the start of a presentation "labels must be rejected" or "*Sentimental Education* was the first modern novel." Friends gave each other books as gifts and wrote dedications on the flyleafs. It was the time of Kafka, Dostoevsky, Virginia Woolf, and Lawrence Durrell. We discovered the *nouveau roman* of Butor, Robbe-Grillet, Sollers, and Sarraute, which we wanted to like, but it didn't offer us enough help with our lives.

We preferred texts with words and sentences that summarized existence, our own and those of deliverymen and cleaning ladies in housing projects, from whom we set ourselves apart because, unlike them, we "asked ourselves questions." We needed words that contained explanations of the world and self, dictated morality: "alienation" and its satellites "bad faith" and "bad conscience," "immanence" and "transcendence." We measured everything in terms of "authenticity." Were it not for fear of quarreling with our parents, who heaped opprobrium in equal measure on divorcés and Communists, we would have joined the Party. In a café one night, as one sat amidst the noise and smoke, the entire setting abruptly lost its meaning. One felt an outsider, without past or future: "a useless passion."

In March the days grew long and our winter clothes too warm. It wasn't only summer that was on its way but life itself, without shape or design. We walked to classes repeating to ourselves: time is out of joint, life is a tale told by an idiot, full of sound and fury signifying nothing. With friends we discussed our preferred method of suicide: with sleeping pills, in a sleeping bag, in the Sierra de Guadalajara.

On Sundays in the mid-1960s, our parents took advantage of the student's presence—home for the weekend with laundry—to invite friends and family to a meal. The table talk revolved around the arrival of a supermarket, the building of a public pool, the Renault 4L and the Citroën Ami 6. Those who had televisions held forth on the physical attributes of ministers and talk show hostesses, discussing celebrities as if they lived next door. The fact of having watched Raymond Oliver prepare pepper steak flambé, a medical program with Dr. Igor Barrère, and *36 chandelles* appeared to grant them a superior right to speak. Before the stiffness and indifference of those who did not have televisions and knew nothing about Zitrone, Anne-Marie Peysson, or the baby doll put through a meat grinder by Jean-Christophe Averty, the others returned to subjects of common interest: the best way to prime rabbit, the benefits of civil servants, and which local butcher shop served the customer best. They spoke of the year 2000, calculated the age they would be and their chances of being alive. They took pleasure in imagining life at the end of the century, with meals replaced by pills, robots doing all the work, and houses on the moon. They did not talk for long, for no one cared how life would be in forty years, *see if we're alive, for starters!*

With a sense of necessary sacrifice—for the guests, who raved about our studies, and our parents, who gave us pocket money and washed and ironed our clothes—of hours one could have spent reading *The Waves* by Virginia Woolf or Stoetzel's *Sociology and Social Psychology*, awkwardly and with good grace, we joined the conversation. We could not help but notice their way of mopping gravy off a plate until it was clean, shaking a cup to dissolve the sugar, uttering the words "a high-ranking person" with a hush of respect, and suddenly we saw the family milieu from the outside as a closed world that was no longer ours. The ideas that possessed us were alien to illness and factory layoffs, vegetables to be planted with the waxing moon, and all the other subjects discussed at the table. Hence our decision not to talk about ourselves and our studies, careful not to contradict them on any subject. To declare we were unsure of getting a good job or teaching later might demolish their beliefs, insult them and make them doubt our abilities.

The company was no longer enraged by memories of the

Occupation and the bombing. No one revived the emotions of yesteryear. When at the end of the meal someone said, "There's another one the Boches won't get," they were simply quoting.

For us too, the great postwar Sundays, *Fleur de Paris* and *Le petit vin blanc* belonged to another time, to childhood, which we had no desire to hear anything about. If an uncle tried to bring it up, "Remember when I taught you how to ride a bike?" we found him old. Immersed in the voices, the words and expressions we'd heard since birth but which no longer came to us spontaneously, we felt ourselves drift on hazy images of other Sundays, back to the times-before whose tales were told when we returned to the table for dessert, out of breath from too much play, and listened to the yarns no one bothered to tell today.

In this black-and-white photo, in the foreground, lie three girls and a boy, on their stomachs; only their upper bodies are visible. Behind them are two other boys. One stands, leaning over, silhouetted against the sky. The other, kneeling, appears to annoy one of the girls with his arm, which is extended. In the background is a valley, submerged in a kind of mist. On the back of the photo: *University Campus. Mont-Saint-Aignan. June '63. Brigitte, Alain, Annie, Gérald, Annie, Ferrid.*

She is the girl in the middle, the most "womanly." Her hair is combed George Sand style in flat bands on either side of a center part. Her broad shoulders are bare, and her clenched fists emerge oddly from beneath her torso. No glasses. The photo was taken during the interval between the sitting of exams and the announcement of their results. It was a time of sleepless nights, long discussions in bars, rented rooms in town, caresses on naked skin, on the point of reckless, and the strains of *La Javanaise*. A time of deep sleeps in the afternoons, from which she emerged with the guilty feeling of having removed herself from the world, as on the day when she awakened to learn the Tour de France and Jacques Anquetil had passed hours before. She joined the party and was bored. The girls on either side of her in the photo belong to the bourgeoisie. She doesn't feel like one of them. She is stronger and more alone. By spending too much time with them, accompanying them to *surboums*, she feels she demeans herself. Nor does she think she has anything in common, not any longer, with the working-class world of her childhood and her parents' small business. She has gone over to the other side but she cannot say of what. The life behind her is made up of disjointed images. She feels she is nowhere, "inside" nothing except knowledge and literature.

At this moment in time, no inventory could be made of the girl's abstract knowledge or of what she has read. The degree in modern literature she is about to receive is only a vague indicator of level. She is a voracious reader of existentialism and surrealism, has read Dostoevsky, Kafka, all of Flaubert, and is also passionate about new writing, Le Clézio and the *nouveau roman*, as if only recent books could provide an accurate view of the here and now.

It seems to her that education is more than just a way to escape poverty. It is a weapon of choice against stagnation in a kind of feminine condition that arouses her pity, the tendency to lose oneself in a man, which she has experienced (see the high school photo from five years before) and of which she is ashamed. She feels no desire to marry or have children. Mothering and the life of the mind seem incompatible. In any case, she'd be sure to be a bad mother. Her ideal is the *union libre* in the poem by André Breton.

At times, she feels weighed down by the quantity of her learning. Her body is young and her thinking is old. In her diary she writes that she feels "hypersaturated with all-purpose ideas and theories," that she is "looking for another language" and "longs to return to an original purity." She dreams of writing in a language no one knows. Words are "little embroidery stitches around a tablecloth of night." Other sentences contradict this lassitude: "I am a will and a desire." She does not say for what.

She sees the future as a great red staircase, the one in a Soutine painting reproduced in the journal *Lectures pour Tous.* She cut it out and hung it on the wall of her residence room.

She sometimes lingers over images of her childhood, the first day of school, a funfair in the rubble, holidays at Sotteville-sur-Mer, etc. She also imagines herself in twenty years trying to remember the discussions of today—everyone's—on Communism, suicide, and contraception. The woman of twenty years from now is an idea, a ghost. She will never live to be that age.

To see her in the photo, a handsome solid girl, one would

never suspect that more than anything, she fears going mad. Only writing—or perhaps a man—can protect her from that, if only momentarily. She begins a novel in which images past and present, her dreams at night and visions of the future, alternate with an "I" who is her double, detached from herself. She is convinced that she has no "personality."

There is no relation between her life and History, though traces of the latter remain fixed in her mind by the gray weather and sensation of cold one March (the miners' strike), by clammy humidity one Whitsun weekend (the death of Pope John XXIII), by a friend's remark, "World war will begin in two days" (the Cuban Missile Crisis), the night at a national students' union dance that coincided with the coup d'état by Generals Salan, Challe, etc. The time of current events, no more than that of sensationalistic news items, which she disdains, is not *her* time, which is wholly comprised of images of herself. A few months later, Kennedy's assassination in Dallas will leave her even more indifferent than the death of Marilyn Monroe had the summer before, because it will have been eight weeks since her last period.

The increasingly rapid arrival of new things drove the past away. People did not question their usefulness, they just wanted to possess them and suffered when they didn't earn enough to buy them outright. They got used to writing checks and discovered the "financial arrangements" available through Sofinco Consumer Credit. Comfortable with novelty, they took pride in using the vacuum cleaner and electric hair dryer. Curiosity prevailed over distrust. We discovered the raw and the flambé, steak tartare and au poivre, spices and ketchup, breaded fish and instant mashed potatoes, frozen peas, hearts of palm, aftershave, and Obao bubble bath. The traditional Coop and Familistère stores made way for supermarkets, where customers delighted in touching the merchandise before paying for it. We felt free. We didn't ask anyone for anything. Every evening, the Galeries Barbès department store welcomed buyers to a free country-style buffet. Young middle-class couples purchased distinction with a Hellem cafetière, Eau sauvage by Dior, a shortwave radio and hi-fi, venetian blinds, burlap wall-covering, a teak living room set, a Dunlopillo mattress, a secretaire or "bureau cabinet," furniture whose names, until then, they had only seen in novels. They frequented antique shops, entertained with smoked salmon, avocado stuffed with shrimp, meat fondues. They read *Playboy*, *Barbarella*, and *Lui*, *Le Nouvel Observateur*, Teilhard de Chardin, *Planète*. They daydreamed over listings for apartments of *grand standing* with walk-in closets, in sparkling new apartment buildings. Hiding their anxiety, they took their first plane trip and were moved to see the green and gold squares below. They lost their tempers with the phone company because they were still waiting for the service they'd ordered a whole year earlier. Others saw no point in having a phone and continued going to La Poste, where the counter clerk dialed the number they were calling and sent them to a booth.

People were never bored. They wanted the full benefit of everything.

In the popular booklet *Thoughts for 1985*, the future seemed bright. Heavy and dirty work would be performed by robots, and everyone would have access to culture and knowledge. We weren't sure how, but the first heart transplant in faraway South Africa seemed to bring us one step closer to the eradication of death.

The profusion of things concealed the scarcity of ideas and the erosion of beliefs.

Young teachers were using the *Lagarde et Michard* from their own high school days, gave out stars for good performance, and assigned term papers. They joined unions, which asserted in every newsletter, "We have the Power!" Rivette's *The Nun* was banned, while erotica could be bought by mail order from the publisher Terrain Vague. Sartre and de Beauvoir refused to appear on television (but nobody cared). Worn-out values and languages lingered on. Later, remembering the nice growly voice of Nounours the bear say *Night-night, children*, we would feel that de Gaulle himself had tucked us into bed each night.

Waves of migration swept through society from every direction. Country people trundled down from mountains and up from valleys. Students were expelled from the city center to campuses in the hills. In Nanterre, they shared the same mud as new arrivals from the shantytowns. OS households and repatriated Algerians left one-story houses with outdoor latrines to be thrown together in housing developments, divided into units marked with an *F* and a number. But communal living was not what people wanted; it was central heating, pale-colored walls, and indoor bathrooms.

The thing most forbidden, the one we'd never believed possible, the contraceptive pill became legal. We didn't dare ask the doctor for a prescription and the doctor didn't offer, especially if one wasn't married—that would be indecent. We strongly sensed that with the pill, life would never be the same again. We'd be so free in our bodies it was frightening. Free as a man.

Young people all over the world were making themselves heard with violence. In the Vietnam War, they saw grounds for revolt and in Mao's Hundred Flowers reasons to dream. There was an awakening of pure joy, expressed by the Beatles. Just listening to them, you wanted to be happy. With Antoine, Nino Ferrer, and Dutronc, zaniness was gaining popularity. Full-fledged adults pretended to ignore it, listening instead to the *Tirlipot* game show on RTL, Maurice Biraud on Europe 1, and Saint-Granier's minute of common sense. They compared the beauty of the television newswomen and discussed whether Mireille Mathieu or Georgette Lemaire would be the new Piaf. The troubles in Algeria had just ended. They were sick and tired of war, and watched uneasily as Israeli tanks mowed down Nasser's soldiers, confused by the return of a situation they had thought settled, and by the transformation of victims into victors.

Because summers had started to be all alike, and caring only for oneself was more and more of a drag, the self-realization imperative taking us nowhere fast, by dint of solitude and discussions in the same cafés; and because youth had come to feel like a vague and cheerless time whose end we could not see, and we'd noted the social superiority of couples over singles, we fell in love more purposefully and, aided by a moment's lack of attention to the Ogino calendar, found ourselves married and soon to be parents. The meeting of an egg and a sperm hastened the unfolding of individual histories. People finished school by taking jobs as monitors, part-time pollsters, and private tutors. A term in Algeria or Sub-Saharan Africa to do community work was tempting as an adventure and a way of fixing a final deadline before one settled down.

Young couples with steady jobs opened bank accounts and took out Cofremca loans to acquire fridges with freezer compartments, dual-fuel ranges, etc. They were surprised to discover that by the grace of marriage, they were poor in the face of all they lacked, the cost of which they'd never guessed, nor the necessity, which now went without saying. Overnight they became adults to whom parents could finally, without fear of rebuke, impart their knowledge of practicalities: saving money, caring for children, washing floors. How proud and peculiar one felt to be called "Madame" with a name not one's own. Sustenance, the twice-daily feeding circuit, became an abiding concern. Diligently we began to patronize places we'd never really gone before, the Casino supermarket, the grocery section of Prisunic, and the Nouvelles Galeries. The vague desire for the carefree kind of life we'd had before—to go to a film or out with friends at night—dwindled with the arrival of the baby. As we sat in the dark cinema, watching Agnès Varda's *Happiness*, he was always on our mind, so little and so alone in his cradle, and we rushed to him the moment we got in, relieved to see him breathing, peacefully asleep with his small fists closed. So we bought a television, thus completing the process of social integration. On Sunday afternoons, we watched *Sky Fighters* and *Bewitched*. Space shrank, time took on a regular rhythm, carved up by work schedules, the day nursery, bath time, *Magic Roundabout*, and Saturday shopping. We discovered the joys of order. Our melancholy at seeing a personal project fade into the distance—painting, writing, or making music—was compensated by the satisfactions of contributing to the family project.

With a swiftness that astounded us, we were forming tiny cells, impermeable and sedentary. Young couples and new parents were invited to each other's homes. Unmarried people, oblivious to monthly bills, tiny Gerber jars, and Dr. Spock, were viewed as an immature species whose freedom of movement vaguely offended.

We never thought to assess our experience in the light of world events or politicians' speeches, but did allow ourselves the pleasure of voting against de Gaulle. Instead we chose a dashing candidate whose name somehow plunged us back into the years of French Algeria, François Mitterrand. In the hum-drum routine of personal existence, History did not matter. We were simply happy or unhappy, depending on the day.

The more immersed we were in work and family, said to be reality, the greater was our sense of unreality.

On sunny afternoons, from their benches in the park, young women exchanged views on diapers and children's nutrition, while keeping an eye on the sandbox. The gossip and secrets of adolescence, when girls interminably walked each other home, seemed very far in the past. That life from before (three years ago at most) seemed unbelievable. They regretted not having taken greater advantage of it. They had entered the Land of Worry over food, laundry, and childhood diseases. They had never imagined resembling their mothers but now were taking up where the latter had left off. They possessed greater levity, offhandedness fostered by *The Second Sex* and *Moulinex Liberates Woman*, but unlike their mothers, they denied the value of things they none-theless felt obliged to do without knowing why.

With the characteristic anxiety and fervor of young mar-ried couples, we invited the in-laws for lunch, to show them how nicely settled we were (and with so much more taste than our siblings). After we'd had them admire the venetian blinds, touch the velvet chesterfield, experience the power of the hi-fi speakers, and brought out the wedding dishes (though a few glasses were missing), when everyone had found a place at the table and commented upon our directions for eating the *fondue bourguignonne*, made from a recipe we'd found in *Elle*, the petit-bourgeois conversation began, about work, holidays, cars, the thrillers of San-Antonio, the length of Antoine's hair, the ugliness of Alice Sapritch, the songs of Dutronc. There was no escaping the discussion of whether or not it was more cost-effective for married women to work outside the home. We made fun of de Gaulle, *Frenchman, I understand you! Vive le Québec libre!* (as if being forced into a runoff by Mitterrand had unleashed the irreverence and revealed the senility of he whom *Le Canard Enchaîné* no longer referred to as anything but "Charles le Run-offed"). We praised the intelligence and integrity of Mendès France and speculated on the futures of Giscard d'Estaing, Defferre, and Rocard. The table buzzed with peacefully disparate and mocking remarks, about the *Barbouzes*,* Mauriac and his stifled cluck of a laugh, the tics of Malraux (to think we'd once imagined him as the revolutionary Chen, whereas now just seeing him in his trench coat at official ceremonies could make anyone stop believing in literature!).

In the mouths of the middle-aged, allusions to the war shrank down to personal anecdotes, full of misplaced vanity, which to the young sounded like drivel. There were commemorative speeches and wreaths for all that, we felt. Names from the Fourth Republic, Bidault, Pinay, brought nothing to our minds except amazement at the loathing they still aroused ("that bastard Guy Mollet"), from which we deduced that

---

* (Slang, pejorative.) Generally, a secret agent, a spook; here meaning anti-OAS agencies who used methods that could not officially be used by the police or the army.

they'd played a role of some importance. As for Algeria, now transformed into mission territory, to the financial advantage of young teachers, the page had turned.

Contraception was too alarming a subject to broach at family meals, and abortion a word that could not be spoken.

We changed plates for dessert, quite mortified that our *fondue bourguignonne* had not been greeted with the expected congratulations, but with curiosity and comments that were disappointing at best, considering the trouble we'd gone to with the sauces, and even a touch condescending. Coffee was served, the table cleared, and a game of bridge set up. The whiskey raised the volume of the father-in-law's voice and thickened his tongue. How was it possible that people still said *Ten thousand English jumped into the Thames for not having trumped.* We sat amidst the new family, saw the faces glowing with contentment, heard the baby crooning, wanting up from his crib, and a sense of impermanence flickered through us. We were amazed to be where we were and to have all that we'd desired, a man, a child, an apartment.

In the photo, taken indoors, a close-up in black and white, a young woman and a little boy sit side by side on a single bed, fitted out with cushions to make a sofa. Behind them is a window with sheer curtains. An African artifact hangs on the wall. The woman wears an outfit in pale jersey, a twin set and a skirt just above the knee. Her hair, parted in dark asymmetrical bands, accentuates the full oval of the face. Her cheekbones are lifted in a big smile. Neither her hairstyle nor her outfit corresponds to the images one later saw of 1966 or 1967. Only the short skirt is consistent with the fashion launched by Mary Quant. The woman holds the child by the shoulder. He is bright-eyed, intelligent-looking, and wears a turtleneck with pajama pants. He is talking and his mouth is open, revealing small teeth. On the back is written *Rue Loverchy, Winter '67*. So the photographer, invisible here, is the student, the flighty kid who in less than four years became a husband, father, and senior administrator in a city in the mountains. It is definitely a Sunday photo, for that is the only day they can be together, and as lunch simmers fragrantly on the stove, and the babbling child assembles Lego blocks, and the toilet flusher is repaired while Bach's *Musical Offering* plays in the background, they build their common store of memory, consolidate their sense, all in all, of being happy. The photo plays a role in this construction, anchoring their "little family" in the long term. It acts as a pledge of permanence for the child's grandparents, who will receive a copy.

At this precise moment of the winter of 1967–68, she is probably not thinking of anything, absorbed in her enjoyment of their self-contained unit of three, which a telephone call or the doorbell would disrupt, and her temporary discharge from tasks whose main object is the maintenance of the unit, shopping lists, laundry counts, what are you making for dinner tonight—an incessant looking-ahead to the immediate future, which complicates the exterior dimension of her duties, her teaching job. In family moments she *feels* rather than thinks.

The thoughts she considers real come to her when she is alone or taking the child for a walk in the stroller. For her, real thoughts do not concern people's ways of speaking and dressing, the height of sidewalks for the stroller, the ban on Jean Genet's *The Screens*, or the war in Vietnam. They are questions about herself, being and having, existence. Real thoughts plumb the depths of transient sensations, impossible to communicate. These are the things her book would be made of, if she had the time to write, but she no longer even has time to read. In her diary, which she rarely opens, as if it posed a threat to the family unit and she were no longer entitled to an inner life, she writes, "I have no ideas at all. I don't try to explain my life anymore" and "I'm a petite bourgeoise who has arrived." She feels she has deviated from her former goals, as if her only progress in life were of the material kind. "I'm afraid of settling into this quiet and comfortable life, and afraid to have lived without being aware of it." Just as she makes this observation, she knows she isn't ready to give up the things this diary never includes, the living-together, the shared intimacy, the apartment to which she eagerly returns after class, the sleeping side-by-side, the sizzle of the electric razor in the morning, the tale of *The Three Little Pigs* at night, the repetition she believes she hates, which ties her down—all the things whose lack she felt when she left for three days to write the CAPES,* and which, when she imagines their accidental loss, make her heart grow heavy.

---

* *Certificat d'aptitude au professeur de l'enseignement du second degré*, the secondary teachers' training certificate. After obtaining their *license* (bachelor's degree), applicants take a one-year course, followed by a probationary year when they work as teachers in training.

She no longer imagines herself lying on the beach or as a writer publishing her first book. The future is laid out in precise material terms: a better job, promotions and acquisitions, the start of kindergarten for the child. These are not dreams but concrete plans. She often revisits images of herself single, in the streets of cities where she has walked and in the rooms she has occupied—in a young ladies' hostel in Rouen, in Finchley as an au pair, or a *penzione* on via Servio Tullio, on holiday in Rome. These are her *selves*, it seems to her, who continue to exist in these places. In other words, past and future are reversed. The object of desire is not the future but the past; she desires to be back in the room in Rome, in the summer of 1963. In her journal she writes: "Out of extreme narcissism, I want to see my past set down on paper and in that way, be as I am not" and "There's a certain image of women that torments me. Maybe orient myself in that direction." In a Dorothea Tanning painting she saw in a show three years before in Paris, a bare-chested woman stands before a row of doors that stand ajar. The title was *Birthday*. She thinks this painting represents her life and that she is inside it, as she was once inside *Gone with the Wind*, *Jane Eyre*, and later *Nausea*. With every book she reads, *To the Lighthouse*, Rezvani's *Les années-lumière*, she wonders if she could write her life in that way too.

She is visited by fleeting images of her parents in the small Normandy town, her mother taking off her work coat to go to evening prayer, her father coming up from the garden with a spade over his shoulder, a slow-moving world that continues to exist, more surreal than a film and far removed from the world in which she lives, modern and cultivated, forward-moving—toward what is difficult to say.

Between what happens in the world and what happens to her, there is no point of convergence. They are two parallel series: one abstract, all information no sooner received than forgotten, the other all static shots.

At every moment in time, next to the things it seems natural to do and say, and next to the ones we're told to think—no less by books or ads in the Métro than by funny stories—are other things that society hushes up without knowing it is doing so. Thus it condemns to lonely suffering all the people who feel but cannot name these things. Then the silence breaks, little by little, or suddenly one day, and words burst forth, recognized at last, while underneath other silences start to form.

Later, journalists and historians would love to recall the words of Peter Viansson-Ponté in *Le Monde* a few months before May '68: *France is bored!* It would be easy to find bleak photos of oneself, full of undatable gloom, of Sundays in front of the TV watching Anne Marie Peysson, and one would be sure things had been that way for everyone—frozen, uniformly gray. And television, with its fixed iconography and minimal cast of actors, would institute a *ne varietur* version of events, the unalterable impression that all of us had been eighteen to twenty-five that year and hurled cobblestones at the riot police, handkerchiefs pressed to our mouths. Bombarded by the recurrent camera images, we suppressed those of our own May '68, far from notorious—the deserted Place de la Gare on a Sunday, no passengers, no newspapers in the kiosks—or glorious—one day when we were afraid of lacking money, gas, and especially food, rushing to the bank to withdraw cash and filling a cart to overflowing at Carrefour, from an inherited memory of hunger.

It was a spring like any other, sleet in April, Easter late. We'd followed the Winter Olympics with Jean-Claude Killy, read *Elise, or The Real Life*, proudly changed the R8 for a Fiat sedan, started *Candide* with the eleventh graders, and paid only vague attention to the unrest at Paris universities, reported on the radio. As usual, we thought, the student rebellion would be quelled by the authorities. But the Sorbonne closed, the written exams for the CAPES were canceled, and students clashed with police. One night, we heard breathless voices on Europe 1. There were barricades in the Latin Quarter, as in Algiers ten years earlier, Molotov cocktails and wounded. Now we were aware that something was happening and did not feel like returning to life as usual the next day. We met by chance and talked, indecisive, and then came together. We stopped working, for no specific reason and with no demands to make, but simply because we'd caught the bug, and when the unexpected suddenly occurs, there is nothing to do but wait. What would happen the next day we didn't know or try to find out. It was another time.

We who had never really come to terms with working and

did not really want the things we bought, saw ourselves in the students, only a few years younger, who threw cobblestones at the riot police. On our behalf, they hurled years of censure and repression back at the State, the violent suppression of the demonstrations against the war in Algeria, the racist attacks, the banning of *The Nun*, and the unmarked black Citroën DS's of the police. They avenged us for our fettered adolescence, the respectful hush of lecture halls, the shame we felt at sneaking boys into our residence rooms. Our allegiance to the blazing nights of Paris was rooted in our crushed desires, the degradations of submission. We regretted we had not seen all this before, but felt lucky it was happening at the start of our careers.

Suddenly, the 1936 we knew from family stories was real.

We saw and heard things we had never seen or heard in our lives, or even thought possible. Places such as universities, factories, and theaters, whose functions were determined by age-old rules and which admitted only specified populations, were now open to all. There, we talked, ate, slept, loved, did everything except the thing for which the place had been intended. Institutional, sanctified spaces were a thing of the past. Professors and students, young and old, company executives and manual workers conversed. Miraculously, hierarchies and distances dissolved into words. We were through with carefully phrased remarks, refined and courteous language, measured tones and circumlocutions, the distance with which, we now realized, the people in power and their flunkies—one needed only watch Michel Droit—imposed their domination. Lively voices spoke with brutal frankness and cut each other off with no apology. Faces expressed anger, contempt, and pleasure. The freedom of attitudes and energy of bodies took one's breath away. If this was revolution, it started there, resplendent, in the expansion and release of bodies that settled themselves anywhere they wanted. When de Gaulle resurfaced—where had he been, we'd hoped he was gone for good—and spoke of *chienlit** with a grimace of disgust, without knowing the meaning we saw the aristocratic disdain for revolt, which he reduced to a word conveying both excrement and copulation, a bestial squirming, the instincts broken free.

We were unconcerned by the absence of an emergent labor leader. With their paternalistic air, the Parti Communiste and union leaders continued to determine needs and desires. They rushed to negotiate with the government, which showed virtually no sign of life, as if there were nothing better to be sought than increased purchasing power and a lower retirement age. At the close of the Grenelle Agreement, as we listened to them pompously outline, in words we'd forgotten three weeks earlier, the "measures" to which the State had "consented," we felt a chill come over us. We began to hope again when the working-class "base" rejected the abdication of Grenelle and Mendès France at Charléty Stadium. The dissolution of the Assembly and the announcement of elections plunged us into doubt again. When we saw the somber crowd unfurl down

---

* A French word dating back to Rabelais, generally meaning "carnival" or "chaos." In de Gaulle's speech of 1968, he pronounced the word as "chie-en-lit," which resulted in a scatological pun. "*La réforme oui, la chie-en-lit non*," literally, *Reform—yes, shit the bed—no*.

the Champs-Élysées with Debré and Malraux, whose inspired and ravaged features no longer saved him from servility, arm-in-arm with the others in a false and cheerless brotherhood, we knew the end had come. There were two worlds and we had to choose between them; it was a fact that could no longer be ignored. Elections were not a choice but simply restored the notables to their former positions. In any case, 50 percent of the young people were not yet twenty-one and couldn't vote. The General Confederation of Labor and the Parti Communiste ordered people back to the lycées and factories. Their spokesmen with their slow, gravelly faux-peasant diction had well and truly shafted us. They were earning the reputation of "objective allies of the State" and Stalinist traitors, an image borne for years to come by union representatives in the workplace, the target of all attacks.

Exams were resumed, trains ran, gasoline flowed anew. People could again go on vacation. In early July, provincial visitors crossing Paris by bus between train stations felt the bump of cobbles, put back in place as if nothing had happened. On their return a few weeks later, they crossed a smooth tarred surface that no longer bumped beneath the wheels, and they wondered where all the tons of cobblestones had gone. It seemed that more had happened in two months than in the ten previous years, but not for us. We hadn't had time to do anything. At some point, we didn't exactly know when, we had missed something, or just let it drop.

Everyone had started to believe in a violent future. It was a matter of months, a year at most. Things would heat up in the autumn, and the spring too, people said (until we eventually stopped thinking about it, and later, coming across an old pair of jeans, we thought, "These did May '68"). Some hoped and worked toward "May Redux" and a new society. Others obsessively feared and resisted it, threw Gabrielle Russier in prison, sniffed out "Leftists" in all young men with long hair, applauded the new antidemonstration law, and condemned everything. In the workplace, people fell into two categories, the strikers and non-strikers of May, ostracized in equal measure. "May '68" became a way of ranking individuals. When we met someone new, we wondered which side they'd been on, though no matter what the camp, the violence had been the same, and we forgave ourselves nothing.

We who had remained with the *Parti Socialiste Unifié* to change society now discovered the Maoists and Trotskyists, a vast quantity of ideas and concepts surfacing all at once. Movements, books, and magazines popped up everywhere, along with philosophers, critics, and sociologists: Bourdieu, Foucault, Barthes, Lacan, Chomsky, Baudrillard, Wilhelm Reich, Ivan Illich, *Tel Quel*, structural analysis, narratology, ecology. From Bourdieu's *Inheritors* to the little Swedish book on sexual positions, everything moved toward a new intelligence and the transformation of the world. Awash in languages hitherto unseen, we didn't know where to start and wondered how we'd remained unaware of it all until now. In a month we made up for years of lost time. It moved and reassured us to see de Beauvoir, in her turban, and Sartre again, older but as pugnacious as ever, though they had nothing new to teach us. André Breton, unfortunately, had died two years too soon.

Now, everything once considered normal had become the object of scrutiny. The family, education, prison, work, holidays, madness, advertising, every aspect of reality was questioned, including the word of the critic, who was ordered to probe his own origins, *where are you coming from, buddy?* Society had ceased to function naïvely. Buying a car, marking a paper, and giving birth all had meaning.

We had to know everything about the planet, the oceans, the crime of Bruay-en-Artois. We had a stake in every struggle, Allende's Chile, Cuba, Vietnam, Czechoslovakia. We evaluated systems and looked for models in an all-encompassing political reading of the world. The key word was "liberation."

Individuals, whether or not they were intellectuals, were entitled to speak and be heard. They needed only represent a group, a condition, an injustice. The fact of having experienced something as a woman, homosexual, class defector, prisoner, farmer, or miner gave one permission to speak in the first person. To think of oneself in collective terms brought a certain exaltation. People spontaneously took the floor, prostitutes and striking workers. Charles Piaget, the factory worker from Lip, was better known than the psychologist of the same name whom our teachers had dwelled upon when we were in Philo (never suspecting that one day, the name Piaget would mean nothing to us but a luxury jeweler advertised in magazines at the hairdresser's).

Boys and girls were together everywhere now. Prize-giving, compositions, and school pinafores were things of the past, numerical scores replaced with letters from A to E. Students kissed and smoked in the schoolyard, declared essay topics *retarded* or *cool!*

We experimented with structural grammar, semantic fields, isotopes, and Freinet's Modern School Movement. We abandoned Corneille and Boileau for Boris Vian, Ionesco, the songs of Boby Lapointe and Colette Magny, *Pilote* magazine and comic-strip books. We wrote a novel or journal that drew on the hostility of colleagues who in '68 had holed up in the staff room, and of parents who raised Cain because we taught *Catcher in the Rye* and *Les petits enfants du siècle.*

We emerged in an altered state from two-hour debates on drugs, pollution, or racism, and in our heart of hearts felt we'd taught the students nothing. Were we not *pedaling next to the bicycle?* And for that matter, was school of any use at all? No sooner had we addressed one question than another leapt into our heads.

In order to think, speak, write, work, exist in another way, we felt we had nothing to lose by trying everything.

1968 was the first year of the world.

On learning of the death of General de Gaulle one morning in November, at first we could not believe it—so we had really believed he was immortal!—and then realized how little we'd thought about him over the past year and a half. His death marked the end of the time before May '68, years that were far behind us now.

Yet as the days went by, marked by the ringing of school bells and the voices of Albert Simon and Madame Soleil on Europe 1, flank steak with fries on Saturdays, *Kiri le clown* and Annick Beauchamp's *A Minute for Women* in the evenings, we perceived no evolution. Perhaps in order to feel it, one needed to stop for a moment, for example, to gaze at the tableau formed by the lycée students sitting on the ground, in the schoolyard, in the sun, after the death of the factory worker Pierre Overney, killed by a security guard at Renault. It was a moment whose distinct flavor was that of a March afternoon, or so we'd thought, but which became, when the time behind us had turned into history, an image of the first sit-in.

The shames of yesteryear were no longer valid. People made fun of guilt, *we are all Judeo-cretins*, denounced *sexual frustration*; *uptight* was the ultimate insult. *Parents* magazine taught frigid women to stimulate themselves with their legs spread in front of a mirror. In a leaflet distributed in lycées, Dr. Carpentier encouraged students to masturbate to fight boredom in class. Touching between adults and children was exonerated. All that had been forbidden, unspeakable, was now recommended. We got used to seeing genitals onscreen but held our breath to contain our emotion when Marlon Brando sodomized Maria Schneider. To improve our erotic skills we bought the little red Swedish book with photos of all the possible positions, and went to see *Anatomy of Love*. We planned to try a threesome someday. But we could not bring ourselves to do what used to be considered indecent exposure, walk naked in front of the children.

The discourse of pleasure reigned supreme. You had to feel pleasure while reading, writing, taking a bath, defecating. It was the alpha and the omega of human activities.

We reflected on our lives as women. We realized that we'd missed our share of freedom—sexual, creative, or any other kind enjoyed by men. We were as shattered by the suicide of Gabrielle Russier as by that of a long-lost sister, and were enraged by the guile of Pompidou, who quoted a verse by Éluard that nobody understood to avoid saying what he really thought of the case. The Women's Liberation Movement had arrived in the provinces. *Le Torchon Brûle* was on the newsstands. We read *The Female Eunuch* by Germaine Greer, *Sexual Politics* by Kate Millett, *Stifled Creation* by Suzanne Hörer and Jeanne Socquet with the mingled excitement and powerlessness one feels on discovering a truth about oneself in a book. Awakened from conjugal torpor, we sat on the ground beneath a poster that read *A woman without a man is like a fish without a bicycle* and went back over our lives. We felt capable of cutting ourselves loose from husband and kids, and writing crude, raw things. Once we were home again, our determination faded. Guilt welled up. We could no longer see how to liberate ourselves, how to go about it, or why we should. We convinced ourselves that our man wasn't a male chauvinist pig. We were torn between discourses, the ones that advocated equal rights for the sexes and attacked "the law of the fathers" versus the ones that promoted everything "female": periods, breast-feeding, and the making of leek soup. But for the first time, we envisaged our lives as a march toward freedom, which changed a great many things. A feeling common to women was on its way out, that of natural inferiority.

We would not remember the day or the month, only that it was spring and one had read from first to last, in *Le Nouvel Observateur*, the names of 343 women who stated they'd had illegal abortions—so many, yet we'd been so alone with the probe and the spurting blood. Even if to do so would be frowned upon, we knew, we added our voice to the others that called for free access to medical abortion and the abolishment of the law of 1920. We printed leaflets on the high school photocopier and slipped them into mailboxes after dark. We went to see *Histoires d'A*, escorted pregnant women to a private apartment where, free of charge, activist doctors performed abortions by vacuum aspiration. A pressure cooker to disinfect the equipment and a bicycle pump with reversed valve was all it took. Dr. Karman had made it simpler and safer to perform the work of the back-street abortionists—"angel-makers," *les faiseuses d'anges*. We provided addresses in London and Amsterdam, exhilarated to be working undercover, as if renewing our ties with the Resistance and the suitcase-carriers of the Algerian War. The lawyer Gisèle Halimi was radiant in the glare of flashbulbs on leaving the Bobigny trial after defending Djamila Boupacha. She too represented this tradition, just as the supporters of *Let Them Live* and Professor Lejeune, who displayed fetuses on television to horrify people, represented that of Vichy. One Saturday afternoon thousands of us marched on the spot with banners, under a blazing sun. We raised our eyes to the cloudless sky of the Dauphiné and told ourselves it was up to us to stop, for the very first time, thousands of years of blood-soaked deaths of women. So who could forget us?

Individuals made the revolution to measure, according to their age, occupation, social class, interests, and old feelings of guilt. Reluctantly they obeyed the orders to celebrate, enjoy without hindrance, and be intelligent, for one must not die stupid. Some smoked grass, lived in communes, went to Kathmandu, joined an *Établissement** group and entered Renault as factory workers, while others spent a week in Tabarka, read *Charlie Hebdo, Fluide Glacial, L'Écho des Savanes, Tankonalasanté, Métal Hurlant, La Gueule Ouverte*, stuck flower decals on their car doors, and in their rooms hung posters of Che and the little girl burned by napalm. They wore Mao suits or ponchos, moved onto the floor with cushions, burned incense, went to see the Grand Magic Circus, *Last Tango in Paris*, and *Emmanuelle*, renovated a farmhouse in Ardèche, subscribed to *Fifty Million Consumers*, where they'd first read about pesticides in butter, went braless, left *Lui* magazine lying on tables in plain view of the kids, who were asked to call them by their first names, like school chums.

---

* Referring to the movement of *Établissement* (the word is not translated into English), primarily practiced by French Maoists. *Établissement* groups were formed by Marxist-Leninist militants, who went to live with the popular masses and work in factories.

They searched for models of existence in space and time, in the exotic or the peasantry, India or the Cévennes. There was an aspiration to purity.

Short of leaving everything, jobs and apartments, to live in the country (a plan constantly postponed but sure to be realized one day), the ones most hungry for rebirth sought remote villages on harsh terrains for holidays. They disdained the beaches where you *tan stupid*, and the home provinces, flat and "disfigured" by industrialization. On the other hand, they credited with *authenticity* poor farmers in arid lands unchanged for centuries. Those who wanted to make History admired nothing so much as its erasure through the return of seasons and immutability of gestures, and from these same farmers bought an old hut for a song.

Or they spent their holidays in an Eastern bloc country. In the gray streets with shattered sidewalks, among the State stores with their penurious no-name stock, wrapped in coarse gray paper, under naked bulbs dangling from the ceilings of apartments lit only at night, they felt they were back in the slow and graceless postwar world of consummate lack. It was a sweet and inexpressible feeling. Yet they would never have wanted to live there. They brought back embroidered blouses and *raki*. They wanted the world to always have countries devoid of progress to take them back in time this way.

In the early 1970s, on summer evenings when the air was heady with the aromas of dry earth, thyme, brochettes, and ratatouille (one couldn't forget the vegetarians), strangers gathered around a big farm table bought from a bric-a-brac trader for barely a thousand francs. The Parisians revamping the house next door, backpackers, hiking enthusiasts, and painters-on-silk, couples with and without children, shaggy men, feral teenage girls, mature women in Indian dresses, reticent at first despite the familiar *tu* (used as a matter of course), struck up conversations on color additives and hormones in food, sexology and body work, anti-gymnastics, the Mezières technique, the Rogers method, yoga, Leboyer's birth without violence, homeopathy and soybeans, self-management, Lip, and René Dumont. They wondered if it was preferable to send children to school or to school them at home, and if Ajax scouring powder was toxic, yoga and group therapy useful, a two-hour workday utopian, and if women should demand equality with men, or equality within difference. They reviewed the best ways to eat, be born, raise children, treat illness, teach, live in harmony with self, the Other, and nature, escape society, and *express oneself*, comparing pottery, weaving, guitar, jewelry, theater, and writing. A vague and immense desire to *create* was in the air. Everyone claimed to be devoted to an artistic activity, or planned to be. All activities were equal, they agreed, and instead of painting or playing the flute, one could always create oneself through psychoanalysis.

All the children were put to bed in the same room and ordered for the sake of form "not to turn the place into a pigsty."

They wreaked havoc with unbridled joy, while the adults drank the moonshine brought by the farmer next door—he'd been invited for the *apéro* only—and talk moved toward brooding sexual questions, were we straight or gay, the first orgasm, confessions. The feral girl declared "I love to shit." Together on that summer evening, these unrelated individuals, cut adrift from family meals and their loathsome rituals, had the exhilarating sense of opening to the world in all its diversity, as if they were teenagers again.

No one thought of bringing up war, or Auschwitz and the camps, or the troubles in Algeria ("case closed"); only Hiroshima, and the nuclear future. Between centuries of peasant life, whose presence one sensed in the fragrant breeze of the *garrigue*, and that night in August 1973, nothing had transpired.

Someone started playing the guitar, singing Maxime Le Forestier's *Comme un arbre dans la ville*, the Quilapayúns' *Duerme negrito*. The others listened, eyes lowered. They would bed down, hit-or-miss, on cots in the former silkworm house, unsure of whether to make love with the neighbor to the right or the one to the left. Before deciding, they were overcome with sleep, euphoric and reassured as to the value of the lifestyle they'd paraded for each other all evening, so far removed from that of the "Joe Six-Packs" crammed into the campsites down at Merlin-Plage.

Now society had a name, "consumer society." This was a certainty, an irrefutable fact whether we liked it or not. An increase in the price of fuel brought things to a halt, briefly. Spending was in the air. There was a resolute appropriation of leisure goods: two-door fridges, gleaming R5s bought on impulse, a week at the Hôtel Club in Flaine, a studio in La Grande-Motte. Television sets were turned in for newer models. The world looked more appealing on the color display, interiors more enviable. Gone was the chilly distance of black-and-white, that severe, almost tragic negative of daily life.

Advertising provided models for how to live, behave, and furnish the home. It was society's cultural monitor. Kids requested fruit-flavored Évian water ("fortified"), Cadbury cookies, Nutella, a slot-load portable record player for listening to songs from the *Aristocats*, remote-controlled cars and Barbie dolls. Parents hoped that all the things they gave their kids would deter them from smoking hash when they were older. And we who were undeceived, who seriously examined the dangers of advertising with our students; we who assigned the topic "Does the possession of material goods lead to happiness?," bought a stereo, a Grundig radio-cassette player, and a Bell & Howell Super-8 camera, with a sense of using modernity to intelligent ends. For us and by us, consumption was purified.

The ideals of May '68 were being transformed into objects and entertainment.

It was disconcerting to see ourselves for the first time on the pull-down screen in the living room. We walked, our lips moved, we silently laughed while the projector sizzled away in the background. We were amazed by ourselves, by our gestures and movements. It was a new sensation, perhaps similar to what people in the seventeenth century felt on seeing themselves in a mirror, or the great-great-grandparents on viewing their first photo-portrait. We did not let on how greatly it disturbed us, and preferred to watch others on screen, relatives and friends, who more resembled what they already looked like to us. It was even worse to hear one's voice on the tape recorder. After that, one could never forget the voice that others heard. We gained self-knowledge and lost spontaneity.

In our clothing (bell-bottoms, tank tops, and clogs), our reading (*Le Nouvel Observateur*), our outrage (at nuclear energy and detergents in the sea), our acceptance (flower children), we felt we were *hip* to our times and therefore sure of being right in every circumstance. Our parents and the middle-aged were from another time, not the least in their very insistence on trying to understand the young. We took in their opinions and advice as pure information. And we would not grow old.

The film's first image is that of a door standing ajar (it is night). It closes and reopens as a little boy comes hurtling out. He stops short, undecided, blinking. He wears an orange jacket and a hat with earflaps. Then a smaller boy appears in a blue hooded anorak with white fur trim. The older child moves restlessly while the other stands frozen, transfixed, as if the film had stopped. A woman enters, wearing a long brown fitted coat, her face hidden by the hood. She carries two cardboard boxes stacked one on top of the other. Grocery items protrude at the top. She pushes the door closed with her shoulder. Disappears from the frame, reappears without the boxes and removes her coat, which she hangs on a "parrot" coatrack. She turns toward the camera with a quick smile, and then looks down, dazzled by the brightness of the magnesium lamp. She is verging on skinny, wears little makeup, brown Karting trousers—close-fitting, no fly—and a brown-and-yellow-striped sweater. Her light brown shoulder-length hair is pulled back with a barrette. There is something ascetic and sad, or disenchanted, in her expression. The smile comes too late to be spontaneous. Her gestures reflect an abruptness of manner and/or nervousness. The children have returned, and stand in front of her. None of the three knows what to do. They move their arms and legs in a group facing the camera, which they gaze at, their eyes now accustomed to the violent light. No one talks. One might almost say they're posing for a photo that will not stop being taken. The bigger boy raises his arm in a grotesque military salute, mouth in a grimace, eyes closed. The camera jumps to elements of the décor that display aesthetic and market value, reveal bourgeois taste: a chest, a hanging lamp made of opaline glass.

Her husband filmed these images when she returned from buying groceries with the children, whom she'd collected after school. The label on the reel reads *Family Life '72–'73*. It is always he who does the filming.

According to the criteria of women's magazines, on the outside she belongs to a growing category of active women in their thirties who juggle work and motherhood, and wish to remain feminine and stylish. A list of the places she goes over the course of a day (the lycée, Carrefour supermarket, the butcher shop, dry cleaner's, etc.), her trips in the Austin Mini between the pediatrician, the older boy's judo club, the little one's pottery class, the post office, and a calculation of time allotted to each occupation—classes and corrections, making breakfast, choosing the children's clothes, laundry, lunch, grocery shopping except for the bread, which he brings home after work—reveals:

—a seemingly unequal division between work inside and work outside the home, paid (two-thirds) and domestic, including child rearing (one-third)

—a wide range of tasks

—a significant frequency of visits to commercial establishments

—an almost total absence of unscheduled time

She doesn't do these calculations—she derives a sort of pride from the quick accomplishment of things that require no invention or transformation—and in any case, they would fail to explain her new state of mind.

She experiences her job as continuous imperfection, a sham. She writes in her diary "Being a teacher tears me apart." Her energy and desire to learn and try new things is boundless. She remembers writing at twenty-two, "If by twenty-five I haven't fulfilled my promise of writing a novel, I'll commit suicide." Would she be happier with another kind of life? The question obsesses her. She wonders to what degree it is a product of May '68, which she feels she missed, having been—already—too settled at the time.

She has started to imagine herself outside of conjugal and family life.

Her student years are no longer an object of nostalgic desire. She sees them as a time of intellectual gentrification, of breaking with her origins. Her memory goes from romantic to critical. Scenes from her childhood often return, her mother shouting *later you'll spit in our faces*, boys wheeling around on Vespas after Mass, herself with the curly perm (as in the photo taken in the school garden), or with her homework spread out on the greasy oilcloth-covered table, where her father liked to "rustle up a snack" (words return too, like a forgotten language), and the things she read (*Confidences*, romances by Delly), the songs of Mariano, memories of academic excellence and social inferiority (the part of the photos that cannot be seen), all the things she has buried as shameful and which are now worthy of retrieval, unfolding, in the light of intelligence. As her memory is gradually freed of humiliation, the future again becomes a field of action. Fighting for women's rights to abortion, against social injustice, and understanding how she has become the woman she is today, are all part of the same endeavor.

Among her memories of the years that have just gone by, she finds none she considers to be an image of happiness:
—the winter of 1969–70, black and white because of the livid sky, and the abundant snow that clung to the sidewalks in gray patches until April; she hunted them down on purpose and smashed them with her boots to help destroy that endless winter, which she associates with the fire at the Saint-Laurent-du-Pont dance hall in Isère, only partly consumed that year and burned to the ground the following winter

—in the square of Saint-Paul-de-Vence, Yves Montand playing *pétanque* in a pink shirt, with a bit of a potbelly, pacing around after every shot, pleased and smug, and eyeing the tourists herded behind barriers, at a safe distance; it was the summer that Gabrielle Russier was thrown in prison and killed herself on returning to her apartment
—the thermal park of Saint-Honoré-les-Bains, the pool where the children sailed toy boats; the Hôtel du Parc, where she lived with them for three weeks, and later confused with the boardinghouse in Robert Pinget's book *Someone*.

In the unbearable part of memory, the image of her father dying, of his corpse in the suit he'd worn only once, to her wedding, carried down from the bedroom in a plastic dustcover because the stairs were too narrow for a coffin.

Political events remain as details only: on TV, during the presidential campaign, the pairing of Mendès France and Defferre, an appalling spectacle, and she'd thought "But why didn't Mendès France run for election alone"; Alain Poher scratching his nose during his last speech before the second round, when she felt that because of that gesture, for everyone to see, he'd be defeated by Pompidou.

She does not feel any particular age, though certainly feels a young woman's arrogance vis-à-vis older women, a condescension toward the postmenopausal. It is unlikely she will ever be one of them herself. She is unperturbed when someone predicts that she will die at fifty-two. It seems to her an acceptable age at which to die.

There were rumors of agitation; things were going to heat up the following spring and in the autumn too. But they never did.

There were committees of high school students, autonomists, environmentalists, antinuclear activists, conscientious objectors, feminists, gays, all the causes blazed but never merged. Maybe there were too many convulsions in the rest of the world, from Czechoslovakia and the interminable Vietnam to the bombing of the Munich Olympics, and one junta after another in Greece. The authorities and Marcellin quietly repressed "Leftist activity." Pompidou suddenly died, and here we'd thought that all he had was hemorrhoids. Union posters in the staff room again announced that the strike of such-and-such a day to protest the "deterioration of our working conditions" would "force the State to retreat." The way we imagined the future was limited to drawing boxes around the days of vacation in our date books, starting from the beginning of September.

Reading *Charlie Hebdo* and *Libération* sustained our belief in belonging to a community of revolutionary pleasure and working, in spite of everything, towards a new May '68.

The "Gulag" brought to light by Solzhenitsyn, and hailed as a great revelation, spawned confusion and tarnished the revolutionary horizon. All over the city, a fellow with an atrocious smile looked out of a poster into the eyes of passersby and said *Your money interests me*. In the end we left things up to the Union of the Left and its joint program, which, after all, we'd never seen until now. Between September 11, 1973, when we marched in the anti-Pinochet demonstrations after the assassination of Allende, while the Right gloated to see the end of "the unfortunate Chilean business," and the spring of 1974, when we watched the televised debate between Mitterrand and Giscard, presented as a great event, we'd ceased to believe there would ever be another May '68. In the following springs, because of balmy rain in March or April, emerging one evening from a parent-student-teacher meeting, we'd have the sense that something could happen, and just as soon feel that it was just an illusion. Nothing happened in the spring anymore, either in Paris or in Prague.

Under Giscard d'Estaing we would live in an "advanced liberal society." Nothing was political or social anymore. It was simply modern or not. Everything had to do with modernity. People confused "liberal" with "free," and believed that a society so named would be the one to grant them the greatest possible number of rights and objects.

We were not especially bored. Even we, who had turned off the TV on election night when Giscard uttered his "I send my cordial congratulations to my unlucky competitor," like so many farts from a mouth tight-pursed as a hen's rear end, were shaken by the new voting age of eighteen, divorce by mutual consent, and debate on the abortion law. We nearly wept with rage to see Simone Veil defend herself alone in the Assemblée against raging men of her own camp, and placed her in our personal Pantheon, next to the other Simone, de Beauvoir, though were distressed by her first appearance on television, in an interview, sporting a turban and scarlet fingernails, fortune-teller style (it was too late, she shouldn't have done it), and ceased to be annoyed when students confused Veil with a woman philosopher we occasionally quoted in class. But we broke for good with the elegant president when he refused to pardon Ranucci, sentenced to death at the height of a summer without a drop of rain—a scorcher, the first in a long time.

Lightness, nods, and winks were in, moral indignation out. We amused ourselves reading the movie billboards for *Suck Divas* and *Little Wet Panties*, and never missed a chance to see Jean-Louis Bory in the role of token "queen." It seemed inconceivable that *The Nun* had once been banned. Still, it was hard to admit how shaken we were by the scene in *Going Places* when a woman's breast is suckled by Patrick Dewaere instead of her baby.

We exchanged the words of current morality for others that measured actions, behaviors, and feelings in terms of pleasure, "frustration" and "gratification." The new way of being was "laid-back," and feeling good about oneself, a mixture of self-assurance and indifference to others.

More than ever people dreamed of country life, away from "pollution," "the rat race," the "métro boulot dodo," "the concentration 'burbs" and the "yobs" who lived there. Still, they flocked to cities, urban priority development zones, and residential suburbs, according to their possibilities of choice.

And we who were under thirty-five grew melancholy at the thought of "digging ourselves in," growing old and dying in the same middle-sized provincial town. Would we ever make it to the place we envisaged as a basin* that shook and rumbled, and pulled us in starting at Dijon, when suddenly the train picked up speed and barreled unstopping, as if possessed, all the way to the gray battlements of the Gare de Lyon. It was the ineluctable trajectory of a successful life, the full attainment of modernity.

The towns of Sainte-Geneviève-des-Bois, Ville d'Avray, Chilly Mazarin, Petit-Clamart, Villiers-le-Bel—those pretty, historic-sounding names that made one think of a film, or the attack on de Gaulle, or nothing at all—could not be found on a map. We only knew they were located within a charmed circle from any point of which one could get to the Latin Quarter and drink a café-crème on Saint-Germain, like Reggiani. One needed only avoid Sarcelles, La Courneuve, and Saint-Denis, with their considerable "foreign population," housed in the "projects" whose "evils" were denounced all the way into school textbooks.

We left. We settled in a new city forty kilometers outside of the Boulevard Périphérique.** A lightweight house in a sub-division nearing completion with the colors of a resort village and streets named after flowers. The doors banged shut with a bungalow sound. Under the sheltering sky of Île-de-France, it was a quiet place at the edge of a field with a line of pylons marching across it.

---

* Geographically, the Paris region is located in a sedimentary basin (*le bassin parisien*).
** The Paris ring road, dividing Paris *intra muros* from the close or inner (*petite couronne*) suburbs.

Farther along were green spaces, glass buildings and government towers, a pedestrian concourse, and other subdivisions linked by bridges over the highway. It was impossible to picture the city limits. We felt ourselves floating in a space too vast. Existence was diluted. It was senseless to go for a walk. As a last resort, we could go for a run in exercise clothes, keeping our eyes straight ahead. Our bodies bore the imprint of the old-style city: streets with cars, people walking on sidewalks.

When we migrated from the provinces to the Paris region, time had started to go more quickly. The sense of time and its passing was not the same. When evening came, we felt as if we had done nothing except perhaps teach some muddled classes to irritated students.

To live in the Paris region was:
—to be cast into a territory whose geography eluded us, scrambled by a maze of roads traveled exclusively by car
—to be unable to escape the goods of leading brands, displayed in vacant lots or along the roads in motley strings of warehouses, on whose outer walls signs touted the oversized and the All—Tousalon, everything for your living room, Worldwide Wall-to-Wall, Leather Galaxy—and suddenly lent a strange reality to the ads on commercial radio, *for home deco and DIY, St. Maclou, of course.*

It was being unable to find a pleasing order in anything we saw.

We were transplanted into another space-time, another world—probably that of the future, which was why it was so hard to define. The only way to experience it was to walk across the concourse at the foot of the Tour Bleue in the midst of people we'd never know and skateboards zinging past. We knew there were thousands of us, millions between here and La Défense, but we never thought of the others.

Here, Paris had no reality. At first, on Wednesdays and Sundays, we had worn ourselves out taking the children to see the Eiffel Tower, the Grévin Wax Museum, and the Seine by tour boat. Historic sites that we had dreamt about as children, and now discovered to be so close on the road signs, Versailles, Chantilly, no longer inspired desire. We stayed home on Sunday afternoons, watching *Le petit rapporteur* and doing home repairs.

The place we went most often, of necessity, was the three-level indoor shopping center, where the air was tepid and sound muted in spite of the crowds. Fountains and benches were arranged under a canopy of glass. Soft-lit arcades contrasted with the pitiless glare of window displays and store interiors. The boutiques were side-by-side with no space between them, so one could come and go without a door to push or hellos and goodbyes to say. Never had clothes and food appeared more beautiful—accessible with no distance or ritual to negotiate. The boutiques with their playful names, The Frockery, Kardkorner, Jean Genie granted a childlike impunity to the act of poking through merchandise. One felt ageless.

It was a different self that did the grocery shopping at Prisunic or the Nouvelles Galeries. From Darty Appliance to Pier Imports, the desire to buy leapt up inside us, as if to acquire a waffle iron and a Japanese lamp would make us a different person, the way that, at fifteen, we'd hoped to be transformed by knowledge of the "in" words and rock 'n' roll.

We slipped into a downy present, unable to say whether it was because of our move to a place without a past, or the infinite horizon of an "advanced liberal society," or a fortuitous conjunction of the two. We went to see *Hair*. In the plane that took the film's hero to Vietnam, we and our illusions from '68 were also sent off to die.

Over weeks and repetitions of the daily circuits, and practice with the parking lots, the sense of strangeness would fade. We would be amazed to find ourselves a part of this huge and nebulous population whose dim roar, rising from the highways morning and night, seemed to imbue us with an invisible and powerful reality. We would discover Paris, locate its streets, arrondissements, and Métro stations, determine the best place on the platform to disembark and transfer to another train. At last we would dare to drive to Place de l'Étoile and Concorde. At the entrance to the Gennevilliers bridge, where the immense vista of Paris suddenly opened up in front of us, we would have the exalted sense of belonging to this huge and hectic life. It was a kind of individual promotion. We would no longer wish to return to what had become for us the undifferentiated "provinces." And one evening, as our train plunged into a night studded with the bright red and blue neon signs of the Paris region, the Upper Savoie city we'd left three years before would seem like the ends of the earth.

The Vietnam War ended. So much had happened in our lives since it began that it was part of our existence. The day Saigon fell we realized that we'd never believed an American defeat possible. They were finally paying for the napalm, the little girl on the poster that hung on our walls. We felt the joy and fatigue of things accomplished at last. But disillusion returned. The television showed clusters of humans clinging to boats to flee communist Vietnam. The civilized mug of debonair King Sihanouk of Cambodia, who subscribed to the *Canard Enchaîné*, could not conceal the ferocity of the Khmer Rouge. Mao was dying and we remembered how, one winter morning in the kitchen, before leaving for school, we heard someone shout *Stalin is dead*. Behind the god of the River of a Hundred Flowers we discovered a band of criminals led by his widow Jiang Qing. Not far from Paris, at the border, the Red Brigades and the Baader-Meinhof Gang kidnapped company presidents and statesmen, later found dead in the trunks of cars, like common mafiosi. It became shameful to hope for revolution, and we didn't dare admit that we were saddened by Ulrike Meinhof's suicide in prison. Through some obscure reasoning, Althusser's crime of choking his wife to death in bed one Sunday morning was blamed as much on the Marxism he embodied as on any kind of mental problem.

The "new philosophers" popped up on television and did away with the old "ideologies." They waved Solzhenitsyn and the Gulag at the revolutionary dreamers to make them cringe. Unlike Sartre, who was said to be senile and still refused to go on TV, or de Beauvoir with her rapid-fire diction, they were young. They challenged our consciences in words that we could understand and reassured us of our intelligence. The spectacle of their moral indignation was entertaining, though it was not clear what they were trying to do, other than discourage people from voting for the Union of the Left.

For us, who as children were enjoined to save our souls with virtuous deeds, in philosophy class to live by Kant's categorical imperative, *act only according to that maxim whereby you can will that it should become a universal law*, by Marx and Sartre to change the world—and who, in '68, had believed that we would—saw no hope in any of it.

The voices of authority were silent on the matter of the troubled suburbs and the families who had just arrived, sharing public housing with others who'd lived there longer and reproached them for not speaking or eating "like us." These were ill-defined and little-known populations who lived a long way off from the idea of happiness that pulled society in like a vacuum cleaner. They'd drawn the short straw, were "disadvantaged," and had no choice but to inhabit "rabbit hutches" where, in any case, no one could imagine being happy. Immigration preserved the face of the helmeted road worker at the bottom of a hole in the highway, or that of the garbage collector beside a dumpster. Theirs was a purely economic existence, triumphantly assigned to them in a virtuous class debate each year by our students, who were convinced they possessed the best of all arguments against racism, i.e.: we need them for work that the French no longer want to do.

Only facts presented on TV achieved the status of reality. Everyone had a color set. The elderly turned it on at noon when the broadcast day began and fell asleep at night in front of the test pattern. In winter, the pious had only to watch *The Lord's Day* to attend Mass at home. Housewives ironed while watching the soap operas on channel 1, or *Madame Today* on 2. Mothers kept children quiet with *Les visiteurs du mercredi* and *The Wonderful World of Disney*. For everyone, TV spelled the availability of immediate, low-cost *distraction* and peace of mind for wives, who were able to keep their husbands home on Sundays with the televised sports. It surrounded us with a constant and impalpable solicitude that bobbed along on the unanimously smiling and understanding faces of the show hosts (Jacques Martin and Stéphane Collaro), their easy affability (Bernard Pivot, Alain Decaux). We were increasingly united by the same curiosities, fears, and satisfactions. Would the heinous murderer of little Philippe Bertrand or the kidnapped Baron Empain be caught? Would the master criminal Mesrine be run to ground? Would the Ayatollah Khomeini regain control of Iran? It gave us a power of quotation that was constantly renewed by current events and news items. It provided information on medicine, history, geography, animals, etc. The bank of common knowledge grew. It was a happy, inconsequential kind of knowledge which, unlike the kind one learned at school, didn't need to be accounted for anywhere but in conversation, as long as one began with *They said . . .* or *I saw on TV that . . .* to indicate distance from the source or proof of veracity, as one chose.

Teachers alone accused television of keeping children from reading and of sterilizing their imaginations. The kids couldn't care less. At the top of their lungs they sang *À la pêche aux moules moules moules*, and imitated the voices of Tweety and Sylvester.

An eclectic and continuous recording of the world was achieved thanks to television. A new kind of memory was born. From the magma of the many thousands of virtual things, viewed, forgotten, and divested of voice-over commentary, items floated to the surface, superimposed—infomercials, faces in the news or generally famous, and strange or violent scenes—so that Jean Seberg and Aldo Moro appeared to have been found dead in the same car.

The deaths of intellectuals and singers added to the bleakness of the times. Barthes's came too soon. Sartre's we'd already thought about and then it happened, majestic. One million walked behind the coffin, and Simone de Beauvoir's turban slipped to the side during the burial. Sartre, who had lived twice as long as Camus, long since laid to rest, along with Gérard Philipe, in the winter of 1959–60.

The deaths of Brel and Brassens, like that of Piaf in the past, were more disorienting, as if we'd expected them to be there for our entire lives, though we didn't really listen to them anymore, one too moralistic, the other an affable anarchist, and preferred Souchon and Renaud. These deaths in no way resembled the ludicrous demise of Claude François, electrocuted in his bath the day before the first round of the legislative elections, lost by the Left when everyone expected them to win, nor that of Joe Dassin, struck down at our own age, more or less, so that all of a sudden, the spring of '75, the fall of Saigon and the surge of hope we associated with Dassin's *L'été indien* seemed very remote.

At the end of the 1970s, at family meals, a tradition maintained in spite of the distances that had to be traveled, memory grew short.

Over coquilles Saint-Jacques and a beef roast from the butcher—*not* from the hypermarket—and a side dish of potatoes *à la dauphinoise,* frozen but as good as homemade, we assured them, the talk turned to cars and brand comparisons, projects for building a home or buying an older property, our most recent vacations, the consumption of time and objects. We instinctively avoided topics that awakened the old social longings and cultural differences, and instead examined the present we shared: the bombings in Corsica, the terrorist attacks in Spain and Ireland, the diamonds of Bokassa, the pamphlet written by a certain "Hasard d'Estaing," Coluche's candidacy for president, Björn Borg, E123 food dye; *La grande bouffe,* which everyone had seen except the grandparents, who never went to movies, and *Manhattan*—just the mainstream. The women managed a sidelong exchange on domestic issues—the folding of fitted sheets, the wear and tear on the knees of jeans, the use of salt to remove wine stains—within a conversation where the men retained the monopoly on subjects.

The recitations of memories from the war and the Occupation had virtually ceased. They were only fleetingly revived over dessert and champagne by the oldest of our number, to whom we listened, smiling, the way we did when they brought up Maurice Chevalier and Josephine Baker. The bond with the past was fading. Only the present was imparted now.

Children were the subject of anxious discussion between parents, who compared child-rearing styles and ways of dealing with permissiveness they had never themselves experienced. They wondered what to prohibit and what to allow (the pill, wild parties, cigarettes, mopeds), weighed the merits of private education, the usefulness of learning German, and language-study holidays. They wanted a good middle school, a good program, a good lycée, good teachers, possessed by the idea of an excellence that would envelop their children and painlessly infuse them with success that the latter would feel was entirely due to their own merit.

The time of children replaced the time of the dead.

When hesitantly asked about their pastimes and favorite music, teenagers replied in a docile manner, laconic and wary, convinced that we were not actually interested in their tastes except as signs of something about them, which they only vaguely perceived—their hidden being perhaps—and which they didn't care to share, or anyway not with us. And, baffled by RPGs, war games, and heroic fantasy, we made sure they quoted *Lord of the Rings* and the Beatles, not just Pink Floyd, the Sex Pistols, and the hard rock they inflicted upon us day and night. When we looked at them, such nice kids with their V-neck sweaters, checked shirts, and sensible haircuts, we felt that for now they were safe from drugs, schizophrenia, and the National Employment Agency.

After dessert, the littlest ones were bidden to show us their artworks created with nails and string, demonstrate their skill with the Rubik's Cube, play Debussy's *The Little Negro* on the piano (to the parents' irritation, no one really listened). We temporized and then decided not to end the family gathering with a card or board game. The young people didn't play bridge, the elders were wary of Scrabble, and Monopoly took too long.

And we, on the threshold of the 1980s, when we would enter our fortieth year, were suffused with a weary sweetness that came of accomplished tradition, and gazed around the table of faces, dark against the light. For a moment we were struck by the strangeness of repeating a ritual in which we now occupied the middle position between two generations. We were overcome with a kind of reverse vertigo, brought on by immutability, as if nothing in society had moved. In the hubbub of voices, which we suddenly perceived as detached from the bodies, we knew that a family meal was a place where one could go mad without warning and push the table over, screaming.

According to one's own desire and that of the State, backed by the banks and household savings plans, couples "achieved home ownership." This dream come true, this social accomplishment, caused time to contract and moved them closer to old age. *Here shall you dwell together till death do you part.* Having sailed through work, marriage, and children, they'd reached the end of the road of reproduction, now etched in stone by twenty years of mortgage payments. They threw themselves into DIY, repainted and wallpapered until their heads spun. They were briefly assailed by a desire to turn back the clock. They envied the young who, with unanimous approval, now practiced a "juvenile cohabitation," which their own generation had not been allowed. All around them, divorce proliferated. They had tried erotic films and lingerie. By dint of making love with the same man over years, women felt they'd become virgins again. The interval between menstrual periods seemed to shorten. They compared their lives to those of singles and divorcées, observed with melancholy a young woman backpacker sitting on the ground outside the train station, peacefully drinking a carton of milk. To test their ability to live without a husband, they went to films alone in the afternoon, quavering inside, and convinced everyone knew they didn't belong there.

They reentered the great market of seduction and were again exposed to the foibles of the world from which marriage and motherhood had removed them. They wanted to go on holiday without husband or children, then realized that the prospect of traveling and being alone in a hotel filled them with anxiety. Depending on the day, they wavered between the desire and fear of leaving it all behind to become independent again.

To find out what we really wanted and boost our courage, we went to see *A Woman Under the Influence* and *Identification of a Woman*. We read *The Left-Handed Woman*, *The Faithful Wife*. The decision to separate was preceded by months of scenes and weary reconciliations, conversations with women friends, hints about marital discord on visits to the parents, who'd issued the warning at the time of the wedding, *In this family, divorce does not exist.*

In the separation process, the inventory of furniture and appliances marked the probable point of no return. A list was made of objects accumulated over fifteen years:
—rugs 300 F
—stereo 10,000
—aquarium 1,000
—mirror from Morocco 200
—bed 2,000
—Emmanuelle armchairs 1000
—medicine cabinet 50, etc.

We fought over them, weighed the market value ("It's not worth anything now") against use value ("I need the car more than you do"). Everything we'd desired together and had been content to acquire when we'd first settled down, things that had vanished into the décor or daily use, recovered their initial and forgotten status of objects with a price. As the list of things to buy, from pots and pans to bedsheets, had once anchored our union in the long term, the list of things to be divided now made the breakup real. It drew a line through shared desire and curiosity, the catalog orders filled out in the evening after supper, the hesitations at Darty Appliance over two models of stove, an armchair's perilous voyage on the car roof, after a garage sale, one summer afternoon. The inventory ratified the death of us as a couple. The next step was to hire a lawyer and translate shared history into legal language, which in one fell swoop purged the breakup of its passion, prodding it toward a banal and anonymous "dissolution of marital community." One wished to flee and leave things as they were, but sensed there was no turning back. One was ready to endure the heartbreak of divorce, the threats, insults, pettiness, and living with half the money, ready for anything that would help us recover the desire for a future.

The color photo of a woman, a boy of about twelve, and a man. They stand apart from each other in triangle formation, their shadows beside them, on a sandy esplanade, white with sun. Behind them is a building that might be a museum. On the right the man, who wears a black Mao-style suit, his back to the camera, arms raised, films the building. From the background, at the tip of the triangle, the younger boy stands looking at the camera. He wears shorts and a T-shirt with an illegible inscription, holding a black object that is probably the camera case. On the left, in the foreground and in semi-profile is the woman. She wears a tight green dress loose at the waist, a style between all-purpose and hippie chic. She holds a thick book that must be the Blue Guide. Her hair is pulled back severely, exposing a rounded face blurred by light. Under the ill-defined dress her lower body appears heavy. Both woman and child seem to have been captured as they were walking, turning at the last moment to smile, alerted by the photographer. The back of the photo is marked *Spain, July '80.*

She is the wife and mother of this little family group, whose fourth member, the teenage son, took the photo. The raked-back hair, drooping shoulders, and shapeless dress, in spite of her smile, indicate fatigue and the absence of a desire to please.

Here in full sunlight, at this unidentifiable place on a sightseeing walk, she probably hasn't a thought for anything outside of the family bubble, a kind of vacuum chamber they walk inside from parador to tapas bar and historic sites marked with three stars in the guide. They take it for rides in the Peugeot 305, whose tires they are afraid to find punctured by the ETA. Inside the bubble, she is momentarily free of the manifold concerns whose elliptical traces can be found in her engagement book—change sheets, order roast, staff meeting (etc.)—and has surrendered to a state of heightened awareness. Since they left the Paris region in the pouring rain, she has tried and failed to shake off her marital pain, a lump of helplessness, resentment, and abandonment. A pain that filters her relations with the outside world. She pays only remote attention to the landscape, simply noting, as they pass the industrial zones on the outskirts of cities, the shadowy hulk of Mammouth on the plain, the disappearance of the little donkeys, and that Spain has changed since the death of Franco. In sidewalk cafés, all she sees is women whom she guesses to be between thirty-five and fifty. She searches their faces for signs of happiness or unhappiness and wonders *how do they do it?* But at other times, from the back of a bar, she watches her children play electronic games with their father, and is devastated by the thought of bringing suffering, through divorce, to such a quiet little world.

From this trip to Spain, the following moments will remain:
—on the Plaza Mayor in Salamanca, as they were having a drink in the shade, she could not take her eyes off a woman in her forties, who could have been taken for an ordinary mother and housewife (flowery blouse, knee-length skirt, a little purse), turning tricks under the arcades
—at the Hotel Escurial in Toledo, wakened by the sound of moaning, she rushed next door to check on the children, who were quietly sleeping. Returning to bed, she and her husband realized it was a woman in the throes of an interminable orgasm, her cries rebounding off the patio walls into all the rooms with open windows. Once her husband had fallen back to sleep, she could not keep from masturbating
—in Pamplona, where they spent three days during the Sanfermines, she napped alone in the afternoon and felt as she had at eighteen in her cubicle at the residence, same body, same solitude, same lack of volition. Lying in bed, she listened to the music meandering through the town, never stopping, with the parade of Giants and Big-Heads.* It was the same old feeling of being outside of the fête.

---

* *Gigantes y cabezudos*, costumed figures that appear in many Spanish festivals and parades.

During that summer of 1980, her youth seems to her an endless light-filled space whose every corner she occupies. She embraces it whole with the eyes of the present and discerns nothing specific. That this world is now behind her is a shock. This year, for the first time, she seized the terrible meaning of the phrase *I have only one life*. Perhaps she already sees herself as the old woman in *Cría cuervos*, the film that shattered her one earlier summer, already so remote, surreal with heat, the summer of the "drought." Paralyzed and mute, her face covered in tears, the woman gazes at photos on the wall while the same songs play over and over again. The films she wants to see and the ones she's recently seen form story lines inside her and she seeks her own life therein— *Wanda, A Simple Story*. She asks them to draw her a future.

She feels as if a book is writing itself just behind her; all she has to do is live. But there is nothing.

We had emerged from our lethargy without noticing.

We viewed society and politics with the joyful derision of Coluche. Children knew all his forbidden sketches and everyone repeated, "It's new, it just came out!" His vision of a France "bent double with laughter" tallied with ours. We were delighted that he wanted to run for president, even if we didn't think we'd go all the way in a kind of sacrilege against universal suffrage by voting for him. We were overjoyed to learn that the disdainful Giscard d'Estaing had received diamonds from an African potentate suspected of keeping his enemies' corpses in his deep freezer. Through a reversal of undetermined origins, it was no longer Giscard who embodied truth, progress, and youth, but Mitterrand, who supported free radio, State-reimbursed abortions, retirement at sixty, the thirty-nine-hour workweek, the abolishment of the death penalty, etc. His new aura of sovereignty was enhanced by his portrait with a village and church steeple in the background, an image of irrefutable fact firmly rooted in old memories.

Out of superstition, we held our tongues. We felt it would bring bad luck to admit our firm belief that the Left would come to power. *Elections are for suckers* was a slogan from another time.

Even as the strange image of Mitterrand formed on the screen from a fragmented pattern of dots, we didn't believe it. Then we realized that we'd spent our whole adult life under governments we didn't care about. Twenty-three years (with the exception of one month of May) that now appeared a hopeless downward slide, devoid of happiness from anything to do with politics. It filled us with resentment, as if something of our youth had been stolen. After all this time, one misty Sunday night in May that erased the failure of '68, we reentered History with a troop of young people, women, workers and teachers, artists and gays, nurses and mail deliverers, and longed to do it all over again. It was 1936, our parents' Front Populaire, the Liberation, a successful '68. We craved lyricism and emotion, the Rose and the Pantheon, Jean Jaurès and Jean Moulin, *Le temps des cerises* and *Les corons* by Pierre Bachelet, stirring words that seemed sincere because we hadn't heard them for so long.

We had to reoccupy the past, storm the Bastille anew, become drunk on symbols and nostalgia before confronting the future. Mendès France's tears of happiness at Mitterrand's embrace were our tears too. We laughed at the terror of the wealthy who hightailed it to Switzerland to stash their money, and condescendingly reassured the secretaries who were convinced their apartments would be seized for nationalized housing. The attack against John Paul II, shot by a Turk, came at a bad time. We'd forget all about it.

Everything seemed possible. Everything was novel. We observed the four Communist ministers with curiosity, as we would an exotic species, amazed that they didn't look Soviet or speak with the accents of Marchais and Lajoinie. We were moved to see members of the National Assembly sporting pipes and goatees, like students from the sixties. The air seemed lighter, life more youthful. Certain words and turns of phrase were coming back, like "bourgeoisie" and "social class." Language ran riot. On vacation highways, we listened at full volume to cassettes of Iron Maiden, the adventures of David Grossexe on Radio Carbone 14, and felt as if a new time were opening up before us.

Never within memory had so many things been granted in so few months (a fact that we would immediately forget, never imagining a return to the previous situation). The death penalty was abolished, the cost of abortions reimbursed, the situation of undocumented immigrants regularized, homosexuality legitimized, vacations lengthened by a week, the workweek reduced by an hour. But the peace didn't last. The government asked to borrow our money. Currency was devalued, controls imposed on rates of exchange, and francs prevented from leaving the country. The atmosphere grew tense, official discourse smacked of punishment ("rigor," "austerity"), as if having more time, money, and rights were somehow illegitimate and we should return to a natural order dictated by economists. Mitterrand no longer spoke of "the people of the Left." We still did not resent him, much. He wasn't Thatcher, who let Bobby Sands die and sent soldiers to be killed in the Falklands. But May 10 became an embarrassing, almost ridiculous memory. National-izations, salary hikes, the reduction of work time, all the things we believed to be the achievement of justice and the advent of a new society, now seemed to have been a vast commemoration ceremony for the Front Populaire, a worship of vanished ideals in which even the celebrants might not believe. The event had not happened. The State was moving away from us again.

It moved closer to the media. Politicians appeared in stage-directed TV shows, made solemn and even tragic with music. They pretended to submit to interrogation and tell the truth. To hear them quote so many figures without hesitation, never in the least surprised, we suspected they'd known the questions in advance; as with school essays, the object was to *convince*. From week to week, they appeared one after another: Good evening Madame Georgina Dufoix, Good evening Monsieur Pasqua, Good evening Monsieur Brice Lalonde. Nothing was retained but a "little phrase" to which we'd have paid no attention if hawk-eyed journalists had not triumphantly put it into circulation.

The facts and reality, material and immaterial, were presented in numbers and percentages, of unemployed, of car and book sales, probabilities of cancer and death, "favorable" and "unfavorable" opinions. *Fifty-five percent of French citizens think there are too many Arabs, thirty percent own a VCR, two million are unemployed.* The figures added up to nothing but fate and determinism.

We could not have said exactly when that obscure and formless entity, the Crisis, became the origin and explanation of the world, the certainty of absolute evil for all. But that is what it was on the day when Yves Montand in a three-piece suit, backed by *Libération* (which had clearly ceased to be Sartre's newspaper), explained that the miracle cure for the Crisis was the Free Market, whose eschatological beauty would later be embodied by the image and voice of Catherine Deneuve for the Bank of Suez, praising its opening to private capital, while the tall sumptuous doors of Money slowly swung open, unlike the ones in Kafka's *Trial*, which they would call to mind.

The Free Market was natural law, modernity, intelligence; it would save the world. (Then, we didn't understand why factories were laying off and closing.) We could expect nothing more from "ideologies" and their "doublespeak." "Class struggle," "political commitment," the opposition of "capital and labor" elicited smiles of commiseration. Some words seemed to have completely lost their meaning through want of use. Others came along and became essential to the evaluation of individuals and actions, "performance," "challenge," "profit." "Success" attained the status of a transcendent value, defined "the France of winners," from Paul-Loup Sulitzer to Philippe de Villiers, and glorified a guy "who started out with nothing," Bernard Tapie. It was the age of the silver-tongued.

We did not believe them. Across from the platform of the Nanterre RER station, near the university, the oversized letters ANPE* on the side of a gray concrete building made our blood run cold. There were so many men, and now women, who panhandled that we concluded it was a new profession. With the credit/debit card, money became invisible.

In the absence of hope, we were given the prescription to "unchain our hearts" with protest buttons, marches, concerts, and CDs to fight hunger, racism, poverty, and to support world peace, Solidarność, the Restaurants du Cœur,** the release of Mandela and Jean-Paul Kaufmann.

The *banlieue*** loomed large in the popular imagination in the shadowy form of concrete blocks and muddy vacant lots at the northern end of the bus routes and RER lines. Urine-soaked stairwells, shattered windows, broken-down elevators, and syringes in the cellars. *Banlieue* youth were in a separate category from other young people, uncivilized and somehow frightening, barely French, even when they were born in France.

---

* The French national employment agency (Agence Nationale pour l'Emploi).
** A charity founded in 1985 by Coluche to distribute food packages and hot meals to the homeless and those of low income. Its activities have expanded since.
*** *Banlieue* (or *banlieues*): in neutral language, suburb or suburbs. Here it specifically refers to the "disadvantaged" suburban zone, equivalent to low-income public housing or "the projects."

Admirable teachers, cops, and firefighters ventured forth to face them down on their own turf. The "intercultural dialogue" boiled down to an appropriation of their way of speaking, an aping of their accent, reversing letters and syllables as they did, saying *meuf* for *femme* and *tarpé* for *pétard* (joint). They had been given a collective name, *les Beurs*, which referred all at once to their origins, skin color, and way of speaking, to which, in derision, an episode of *Je-parle-France* had been devoted. There were a lot of them. We didn't know them.

A figure from the extreme Right, Jean-Marie Le Pen, made a comeback. We recalled seeing him years ago with a black band over one eye, like Moshe Dayan.

On the outskirts of cities, covered markets and gigantic warehouses, open on Sundays, flogged shoes, tools, and home furnishings by the thousands. Hypermarkets expanded, shopping carts were replaced by others so big that one could scarcely touch the bottom, short of leaning all the way over. We changed television sets so that we could acquire a SCART connector and a VCR. People were soothed by the arrival of the new. The certainty of continuous progress removed the desire to imagine it. New objects were no longer met with wonder or anxiety, but welcomed as additions to individual freedom and pleasure. CDs removed the need to get up every fifteen minutes to flip a record over, and thanks to the remote control one did not have to leave the couch all evening. Videotapes made the great home-cinema dream come true. On the Minitel, we checked phone listings and train schedules, horoscopes and porn sites. Now we were free at last to do everything at home—no need to ask anyone for anything. Genitals and sperm could be viewed in close-up without shame. The sense of surprise was fading. People forgot there'd been a time when they never thought they'd see the like. But there it was. One saw. And then, nothing. Only the satisfaction of having access, with complete impunity, to once-forbidden pleasures.

With the Walkman, for the first time music entered the body. We could live inside music, walled off from the world.

The young were sensible. For the essentials, they shared our way of thinking. They didn't heckle us at the lycée, challenge the curriculum, the rules, or authority, and accepted the boredom of classes. Outside of school they came to life. They spent hours at a time on Playstations or Atari consoles, and playing role-playing games. They raved about home computers and begged us to buy the first model, Oric-1. They watched *Les enfants du rock, Les Nuls,** nonstop music videos on *Bonsoir les clips,* read Stephen King and to make us happy, leafed through

---

* *Les enfants du rock* ("the children of rock," 1982 to 1988): weekly pop culture TV "magazine," showcasing vanguard rock, comics, film, etc.
Les Nuls (meaning "the boneheads"): a group of French comedians and their eponymous TV show (1987 to 1992, Canal+), filmed live, with a guest host, skit-based and sometimes compared to *Saturday Night Live.*
.

the *Phosphore*, the lycée students' magazine. They listened to funk and hard rock, or rockabilly. Between LPs and Walkmans, they lived inside music. They "partied hard" at *teufs* and probably smoked *tarpés*. Studied. Were close-mouthed about their futures. Opened the fridge and cupboards at all hours to eat Danette pudding cups, Bolino instant noodles, and Nutella. Slept with their girlfriends at our apartment. They didn't have time for everything, sports, painting, film club and school trips. They didn't resent us for anything. Journalists referred to them as the *whatever* generation.

Schooled together since kindergarten, girls and boys grew up quietly in what seemed to us a kind of innocence and equality. They all spoke the same crude, ill-mannered language. They called each other assholes and told each other to fuck off. We found them "very much themselves" and "natural" in relation to all that had tormented us at their age, sex, teachers, parents. We questioned them with circumspection, afraid they'd say we were a pain in the ass and got up their noses. We allowed them a freedom we'd have loved to have had ourselves, but discreetly watched over their behavior and silences, as our mothers had done with us. We looked upon their autonomy and independence with surprise and satisfaction, as something that had been won over several generations.

They had a thing or two to teach us about tolerance, antiracism, pacifism, and ecology. They weren't interested in politics but adopted all the generous watchwords and the slogan created just for them, *Touche pas à mon pote!** They bought the CD

---

* Slogan of the SOS Racisme organization, founded in 1984 in France. Its logo is a hand with the slogan *Touche pas à mon pote*, meaning "Hands off my buddy!"

for hunger relief in Ethiopia, followed the march of the *Beurs*. They proved to be exacting about the "right to be different." They had a moral worldview. We liked them.

At holiday lunches, references to the past were few and far between. For the younger people there seemed no point in exhuming the grand narrative of our entry into the world, and we loathed wars and hatred as much as they did. We didn't bring up Algeria, Chile, Vietnam, May '68, or the fight for free abortion. Our children were our only contemporaries.

The time-before vanished from family tables, and fled the bodies and voices of its witnesses. It appeared on television in documentary archives with commentary by voices that came from nowhere. The "duty of remembrance" was a civic obligation, the sign of a just conscience, a new patriotism. For forty years we'd consented to indifference about the genocide of the Jews—one could not say that *Night and Fog* had drawn crowds, nor the books of Primo Levi and Robert Antelme—and thought we felt shame, but it was delayed shame. Only in watching *Shoah* did conscience contemplate in horror the extent of its own potential for inhumanity.

Genealogy was all the rage. People went to the town halls in their native regions and collected birth and death certificates. They were fascinated, and then disappointed by mute archives where nothing appeared but names, dates, and professions: Jacques-Napoléon Thuillier, born July 3, 1807, day laborer; Florestine-Pélagie Chevalier, weaver. We clung to photos and family objects, amazed to think of how many we'd lost in the seventies without regret, whereas we missed them so much today. We needed to "re-source" ourselves. The "roots" imperative prevailed.

Identity, which until then had meant nothing but a card in one's wallet with a photo glued onto it, became an overriding concern. No one knew exactly what it entailed. Whatever the case, it was something you needed to have, rediscover, assume, assert, express—a supreme and precious commodity.

There were women in the world who were veiled from head to toe.

The body, whose "fitness" was maintained through jogging, *Gymtonic*, and aerobics, its inner purity with Évian water and yogurt, pursued its voyage toward Assumption. The body did our thinking. Sexuality had to be "fulfilled." We read Dr. Leleu's *Treaty on Caresses* to perfect our skills. Women wore stockings, garter belts, and corsets again, and claimed it was "mainly for themselves." The injunction to "pamper oneself" came from every quarter.

Couples in their forties watched X-rated films on Canal+. Faced with indefatigable cocks and shaved vulvas in close-up, they were seized by a kind of technical desire, a distant spark compared to the conflagration that propelled them together ten or twenty years before, when they didn't even have time to remove their shoes. At the moment of climax they said "I'm coming" like the actors on Canal+. They fell asleep with the satisfied feeling of being normal.

Hopes and expectations moved away from things toward the preservation of the body, unalterable youth. Health was a right, and illness an injustice to be remedied as swiftly as possible.

Children no longer had worms and hardly ever died. Test-tube babies were common and the worn-out hearts and kidneys of the living were replaced by those of the dead.

Shit and death had to be invisible.

We preferred not to talk about the "new" diseases that had no cures. The one with the Germanic name, Alzheimer, which made the old look crazed and forget names and faces. The other was contracted through sodomy and syringes, a punishment for homosexuals and drug addicts, or in rare cases, dumb bad luck for recipients of blood transfusions.

The Catholic religion had unceremoniously vanished from our lives. Families no longer imparted its teachings or its practices. With the exception of certain rites, it was no longer required as a sign of respectability, as if it had been overused, worn out by billions of prayers, masses, and processions over two millennia. Venial and mortal sins, the commandments of God and the Church, grace and theological virtues belonged to an unintelligible vocabulary, an obsolete mind-set. Sexual freedom had made lust as sin passé, along with naughty stories about nuns and the raunchy ballads of the Curé de Camaret. The Church no longer terrorized the teenage imagination or ruled over sexual exchange. Women's bodies were freed from its clutches. By losing sex, its main field of endeavor, the Church had lost everything. Outside of philosophy courses, the idea of God was neither indisputably valid nor a serious matter for debate. A student had carved in a table at the high school, *God exists I stepped in him.*

The celebrity of the new Polish pope changed nothing. He was a political hero of Western freedom, a world-class Lech Walesa. His Eastern European accent and white robe, his way of saying "Do not be afraid" and kissing the earth when he got off the plane, were all part of the show, like the throwing of panties at Madonna concerts.

(Convent school parents had marched together one hot Sunday in March, but everyone knew that it had nothing to do with God. It was a matter of faith, but secular rather than religious. It had to do with certainty about a product that guaranteed their children's success.)

It is a thirty-minute videotape, recorded in a tenth-grade class at a lycée in Vitry-sur-Seine, in February 1985. She is the woman who sits the table, the kind of table one saw in all the schools as of the 1960s. Students sit across from her on chairs in haphazard groupings. Most are girls. Several are African, North African, and West Indian. Some wear makeup, low-cut sweaters, gypsy earrings. In a slightly high-pitched voice, she talks about writing, life, and the status of women, with hesitations, cuts and retakes, especially when a question is asked. She seems overwhelmed by the need to take everything on board, as if assailed by a whole that she alone perceives, and then suddenly utters a sentence of no particular originality. She moves her hands, which are large, often raking them through her mass of red hair, but there is none of the nervousness and jerky movements seen in the Super-8 home movie of thirteen years before. Compared to the photos from Spain, the cheekbones are less prominent while the jaw-line and oval of the face are more sharply defined. She laughs. It's a light little laugh that just slips out—shyness, or the vestige of a giggly, working-class adolescence, the attitude of a young girl who acknowledges her lack of importance—and contrasts with the calm and gravity of her face in repose. She wears little makeup, no powder (her skin is shiny), a red scarf slipped into the opening of a tightly buttoned bright green shirt. Her lower body cannot be seen because of the table. No jewelry. One of the students asks:

When you were our age, how did you imagine your life? What did you hope for?

The answer (slowly): I'd have to think about it . . . to go back to being sixteen, to be sure . . . would take at least an hour. (The voice is suddenly high-pitched, edgy.) You live in 1985, women can choose to have children if they want, when they want, out-side of marriage. Twenty years ago that was impossible!

No doubt she feels discouraged by this "communication sit-uation" as she measures her inability to impart through some other means than stereotypes and commonplace words the full reach of a woman's experience between the ages of sixteen and forty-four. (She would have to immerse herself in photos from the tenth grade, find songs and notebooks, reread diaries.)

At this point in her life she is divorced, lives with her two sons, and has a lover. Of necessity, she has sold the house and the furniture bought nine years earlier, with an indifference that surprised her. She's in a state of material dispossession and freedom. As if the marriage had only been an interlude, she feels she's picked up the thread of her adolescence where she'd left it off, returning to the same kind of expectancy, the same breathless way of running to appointments in high heels, and sensitivity to love songs. It is a return to the same desires, too, but now she is not ashamed to satisfy them to perfection, capable of saying I want to fuck. The reversal of values from before '68 is already remote; now it is in her body's imperious acquiescence that the "sexual revolution" unfolds, and in her own awareness of the fragile splendor of her age. She's afraid of getting old. She's already afraid of missing the scent of the blood that one day will cease to flow. Recently, an official letter had informed her that her current position was effective until the year 2000. It had left her transfixed. Up until now, that date has had no reality.

Her children are not usually present in her thoughts, no more than her parents were when she was a child and a teen. They are a part of her. Because she's no longer a wife, she's not the same mother, more a combination of sister, friend, counselor, and organizer of a daily life that has grown lighter since the separation. Everyone eats when they want to, from a tray balanced on their knees in front of the TV. She often looks at them in amazement. So all the waiting for them to grow up, the grain-and-honey Pablum, the first day of first grade and later of middle school, have produced these big boys, whom she suspects she knows very little about. Without them she would be unable to locate herself in time. When she sees small children playing in a sandbox, she's amazed to find that she already looks back on her own sons' childhoods, which seem very far in the past.

The important moments of her current existence are the meetings with her lover in the afternoon at a hotel on rue Danielle-Casanova, and the visits to her mother at the hospital in long-term care. For her, these meetings and visits are so very intertwined they sometimes seem to revolve around a single being. As if caressing the skin and hair of her lost mother were the same kind of touch as the erotic gestures of her afternoons with her lover. After love, she nestles into his massive body; there is traffic noise in the background, and she recalls other times she has curled up this way in the daytime: on Sundays in Yvetot as a child, as she read against her mother's back, in England as an au pair girl, wrapped in a blanket next to an electrical heater, and in the Maisonnave hotel in Pamplona. Each time, she'd had to leave this gentle state of torpor, get up, do homework, go down to the street, socially exist. At these moments she thinks that her life could be drawn as two intersecting lines: one horizontal, which charts everything that has happened to her, everything she's seen or heard at every instant, and the other vertical, with only a few images clinging to it, spiraling down into darkness.

Because in her refound solitude she discovers thoughts and feelings that married life had thrown into shadow, the idea has come to her to write "a kind of woman's destiny," set between 1940 and 1985. It would be something like Maupassant's *A Life* and convey the passage of time inside and outside of herself, in History, a "total novel" that would end with her dispossession of people and things: parents and husband, children who leave home, furniture that is sold. She is afraid of losing herself in the profusion of objects that are part of reality and must be grasped. And how would she organize the accumulated memory of events, and news items, and the thousands of days that have conveyed her to the present?

Already, at this distance, all that remains of May 10, 1981, is the image of a middle-aged woman slowly walking her dog in the empty street, whereas exactly two minutes later, all the television and radio stations would announce the name of the next president of the Republic, and Rocard would pop up on the screen like a Cartesian diver, Everyone to the Bastille!

And from the recent past:
—the death of Michel Foucault from septicemia, according to *Le Monde*, at the end of June, before or after the massive cultural event at the convent school, a sea of pleated skirts and white blouses; two years earlier, the death of Romy Schneider, whom she saw for the first time in *Sissi the Young Empress*, but only in snippets, the screen blocked by the head of the boy who was kissing her in the back row of the theater, traditionally allotted to this purpose
—the truckers who blocked the roads on the eve of the February vacation
—the steelworkers—whom she associated with the workers from Lip—who burned tires on the train tracks, and she read *The Order of Things* in her seat on the immobilized TGV

People sensed that nothing could prevent the return of the Right in the next elections, that the fate of the opinion polls had to be fulfilled, and the unknown situation of "cohabitation" inexorably occur, like an unspoken desire the media loved to inflame. The government of the Left seemed to keep doing the wrong thing every time, the TUC jobs for youth,* the elegant Fabius snubbed by Chirac on TV, Jaruzelski in mafioso sunglasses received at the Élysée, the sabotage of the *Rainbow Warrior*. Even the hostage taking in Lebanon, a new chapter in a conflict no one understood, came at the wrong time. We were irked by the nightly behest not to forget that Jean-Paul Kaufmann, Marcel Carton, and Marcel Fontaine were still being held hostage—what were we supposed to do about it? Depending on which side they were on, people were distressed or up in arms. Even the colder than usual winter—snow in Paris, thirteen degrees Fahrenheit in the Nièvre—bode no good. The hush of AIDS deaths and its ravaged survivors was all around us. We were in a state of mourning. Every evening when Pierre Desproges closed his *Chronique de la haine ordinaire* with "As for the month of March, and I say this with no political bias, I'll be surprised if it lasts the winter," we understood it was the Left that would not survive the winter.

---

* TUC jobs (*travail d'utilité communataire*): part-time jobs, actually "internships" of a six-month (maximum) duration, in public institutions, for young job seekers. Paid less than half the minimum wage, the jobs were ineligible for social benefits, and presented no possibility of advancement.

The Right came back and resolutely undid all that had been done. It denationalized, abolished the official permission requirement for dismissal, and the wealth tax, none of which were making enough people happy. We liked Mitterrand again.

Simone de Beauvoir died, and Jean Genet, no, we definitely did not like that April, moreover snow continued to fall in Île-de-France. We didn't like May either, though were not unduly disturbed by the nuclear power plant explosion in the USSR. A catastrophe the Russians had failed to hide, surely the result of their incompetence, and inhumanity commensurate with the Gulag (though Gorbachev seemed a nice enough fellow), but it didn't affect us. One sultry afternoon in June, students emerged from their *bac* exams to learn that Coluche had been killed riding his motorcycle down a quiet road.

The wars in the world followed their due course. Our interest in them was inversely proportional to their duration and the distance from where we lived. It especially depended on whether Westerners were involved. We couldn't have said how many years the Iranians and Iraqis had been killing each other, or the Russians trying to subdue the Afghans, let alone the reasons why, firmly convinced that they didn't know either. We halfheartedly signed petitions related to conflicts whose causes we'd already forgotten. We confused the warring factions in Lebanon: Shiites, Sunnis, and Christians as well. That people could murder each other over religion was beyond our comprehension. It seemed to prove that these populations had remained at an earlier stage of evolution. We were through with the idea of war. We no longer saw boys in uniform in the street, and military service was a burden that everyone tried to escape. Anti-militarism had lost its reason for being. Boris Vian's *Le déserteur* alluded to another era. We would have been happy to see blue berets everywhere so peace would reign eternal. We were civilized, increasingly concerned with hygiene and personal grooming, users of products that rid our bodies and homes of nasty odors. We joked, "God is dead, Marx is dead, and I don't feel so good either." We had a sense of play.

Isolated acts of terrorism, whose perpetrators disappeared and roamed the earth, like Carlos, scarcely moved us. We may not have remembered the first attacks of September, just after school began, if other bombs had not gone off in public places at a few days' interval, leaving us no time to emerge from stupor and television no time to exhaust one attack before the next one occurred. Later we will wonder when exactly we started to think that an invisible enemy had declared war on us, and will recall rue de Rennes on that Wednesday afternoon, so hot. We'll remember the immediate calls to family and friends to reassure ourselves they hadn't been among the people killed by the bomb hurled from a passing BMW at a Tati store. People continued to take public transport, but the air in the Métro and RER cars silently thickened. As we took our seat, we eyed the sports bags at the feet of "suspicious" passengers, especially those who could be said to belong to the group that was implicitly designated as guilty of the attacks, i.e., Arabs. Suddenly, with the awareness of imminent death, we felt our bodies and present time with violent intensity.

We expected further bloodshed, convinced that the government could not prevent it. Nothing happened. As days went by, we ceased to be afraid and to check under seats. The explosions had suddenly stopped and we didn't know why, any more than we knew why they had started, and in any case were so relieved that we gave it no more thought. The attacks of what had become "the week of blood" did not constitute an event, and had not changed the lives of the greater number, except in the way we felt out in the streets and public places, a sense of anxiety and fatality that disappeared as soon as the danger had subsided. We did not know the names of the dead and wounded, who formed an anonymous category with the name "the victims of the September attacks," with a subcategory, "the victims of rue de Rennes," more specific because more had died and it is even more dreadful to die in a street one was only passing through. (Obviously we would be more familiar with the names of Georges Besse, the CEO of Renault, and General Audran, mowed down by a splinter group called Action Direct, whom we felt had got their decades mixed up and followed the lead of the Red Brigades and Baader-Meinhof.)

Two months later, because it had happened before and we had been there for it, we thought a true event had begun when university and lycée students took to the streets to protest the Devaquet Law. We marveled, we hardly dared hope. May '68 in winter—for us it was the fountain of youth. But youth put us in our place. Their banners read *68: passé, 86: the better way*. We didn't hold it against them. They were good kids. They didn't throw cobblestones and expressed themselves sedately on TV.

In the demonstrations they charmed us with couplets sung to the tune of *Petit navire* and *Pirouette cacahuète*. You had to be Pauwels and *Le Figaro* to say the kids were suffering from "AIDS of the brain." For the first time, we saw the next generation in its huge and daunting reality, the girls on the front lines with the boys and the *Beurs*, and all of them in jeans. Their great number made them adults—were we so old already? A boy of twenty-two, who in photos looked like a child, died under the blows of the riot police in rue Monsieur-le-Prince. In a somber crowd of thousands, we marched behind banners emblazoned with his name, Malik Oussekine. The government withdrew the law, the protesters returned to university and high school. They were pragmatic. Their goal was not to change society. They simply didn't want their chances ruined of acquiring good positions within it.

And we, who knew very well that a "secure profession" and money didn't necessarily bring happiness, couldn't help but want happiness for them.

Cities sprawled farther and farther into the countryside, which was soon dotted with new pink villages. There were no vegetable gardens or chicken runs, and dogs were forbidden to roam free. The landscape was crosshatched with highways that tangled around Paris in a kind of aerial figure eight. People passed more and more hours in quiet and comfortable cars with big windows and music. It was a kind of transitory housing, increasingly personal and familial, where strangers were not admitted (hitchhiking was a thing of the past) and people sang, quarreled, told secrets with their eyes on the road, not the passenger, and reminisced. Cars were spaces at once open and closed. Other motorists were reduced to a flash of profile as we passed them, bodiless beings whose sudden reality in accidents, as broken marionettes slumped in their seats, filled us with horror.

When we drove alone at the same speed for a long time, the familiar gestures grew automatic and we ceased to feel our bodies, as if the car were driving itself. Valleys and plains slipped by in a spacious, rounded movement. We were nothing but a gaze in a cockpit, transparent to the end of the moving horizon, a huge and fragile consciousness that filled inner space and the entire world beyond it. All it would take, we sometimes told ourselves, was for a tire to explode or an obstacle to appear on the road, as in Sautet's film *The Things of Life*, for consciousness to vanish forever.

Media time, ever more frenetic, forced us to think about the presidential elections, counting down the months and then the weeks that remained. People preferred to watch the menagerie on TF1's *Bébête Show*, reviled by the highbrow, and *Les Nuls* on Canal+, "coarse but never vulgar" according to a distinction currently in vogue, or dreamed of their next vacation, listening to Desireless sing *Voyage voyage*. It was quite enough that you had to be afraid of making love, now that everyone knew AIDS was not only a disease of homosexuals and drug addicts, contrary to what one had first believed. Between the end of pregnancy scares and the onset of HIV scares, the interval of calm had seemed short-lived.

In any case, compared to '81, our hearts were no longer in it. We had neither expectations nor hopes, only a desire to keep Mitterrand in and Chirac out. Mitterand was reassuring, the favorite uncle, a man of the Center surrounded by yuppie ministers from whom the people of the Right feared nothing anymore. The Communist Party was running out of steam. Gorbachev's perestroika and glasnost had aged him. He was stuck in the Brezhnev era. Le Pen was omnipresent; there was no getting around him. He drew the fascination and terror of journalists with a gravitational pull. For half the population he was "the guy who said out loud what others were secretly thinking," i.e., there were too many immigrants.

Mitterrand's reelection restored our tranquillity. Far better to live without expectations under the Left than in constant fury under the Right. In the irreversible flow of time, this election would not be earth-shattering but only a backdrop to a spring, when we learned of Pierre Desproges's death from cancer, and laughed more than we had in a long time at the Groseilles and Le Quesnoy families in a film that seemed tailor-made to incite people to vote for Mitterrand. We would barely remember adjacent events, which came at an opportune time—the release of the hostages in Lebanon, that interminable saga, and the massacre of Kanaks in the Ouvéa cave—or the TV debate in which Chirac insisted Mitterrand look him in the eye and swear that a probable lie was true. We were worried, and then relieved to see that true to form, Mitterrand didn't flinch.

Nothing happened but an accommodation of poverty with the minimum guaranteed income, and a promise to repaint the stairwells in the housing projects, an adjustment to the lives of a population large enough to receive the denomination of "underclass." Charity was becoming institutionalized. Panhandling vacated the major cities for provincial supermarkets and beaches in the summer. New techniques were invented, kneeling with the arms crossed, the discreet soliciting of change with a hushed voice, and new pitches that grew shabby faster than plastic grocery bags, themselves emblematic of dereliction. The homeless were as much a part of the urban landscape as advertising. People grew discouraged—too many poor—and irritated at their own powerlessness—how can you give to everyone?—and found relief in quickening their pace in Métro corridors when passing recumbent bodies, whose utter lack of movement served as obstacles to their purposeful advance. On the State radio, industry groups sent out celestial messages, *Welcome to the world of Rhône-Poulenc, a world of challenge*, and we wondered whom they could possibly be talking to.

We looked elsewhere. The Imam Khomeini pronounced a death sentence on Salman Rushdie, a writer of Indian origin whose only crime was having offended Mohammed in a novel. The news traveled around the planet and left us dumbfounded. (The pope also pronounced a death sentence by prohibiting the condom but those were deferred and anonymous deaths.) And so, three girls who persisted in wearing headscarves to school were perceived as the advance guard of Muslim fundamentalism, obscurantist and misogynistic, and finally provided us with an opportunity to think and suggest that the Arabs were not like other immigrants. We started to see ourselves as too nice for our own good. Rocard had already removed a burden from innumerable consciences when he declared, "France cannot take on all the misery of the world."

The new came from the East. The magical words "perestroika" and "glasnost" had never ceased to enchant us. The Gulag and the tanks of Prague forgotten, our image of the USSR changed. We noted signs of their resemblance with ourselves, and the West in general: freedom of the press, Freud, rock and jeans, haircuts and the beautiful suits the "new Russians" wore. We waited, indeed hoped, for some kind of fusion between Communism and Democracy, the market economy and Lenin's planning. We longed for an October Revolution with a happy ending. We warmed to the Chinese students with their little round metal-rimmed glasses who gathered in Tiananmen Square. And we believed in their victory until the tanks suddenly appeared (not them again!). A young man stepped forward, alone and tiny—that image we would see dozens of times, like the last sublime image of a film—on the same Sunday that Michael Chang won the final at Roland-Garros, with the result that the student of Tiananmen Square merged with the tennis player, though we found Chang so irritating with his repeated signs of the cross.

On the evening of July 14, 1989, at the end of a gray day of heat, we sat on the chesterfield and watched Jean-Paul Goude's cosmopolitan fashion show, with voice-over commentary by Frédéric Mitterrand. We had the impression that all the world's

revolts and revolutions were our handiwork, from the eradication of slavery to the shipyards of Gdańsk and Tiananmen
Square. There before us were all the peoples of the earth, every
struggle of the past, present, and future, all progeny of the
French Revolution. When Jessye Norman sang *La Marseillaise,*
her dress of *bleu-blanc-rouge* rippling in the artificial wind, we
were seized by an emotion at once ancient and scholastic, a
surge of glory and History.

The East Germans crossed borders, swarmed around churches
with candles to bring down Honecker. The Berlin Wall fell.
What followed was a short-lived epoch when tyrants were exe-
cuted after an hour's trial, and soil-covered corpses were exposed
in mass graves. What was happening defied the imagination—so
we really had believed that Communism was immortal—and
our were at odds with reality. We felt left out, and envied the
people in the East for experiencing such moments. Then we saw
them crowding into the stores of West Berlin, and they moved us
to pity with their awful clothes and bags of bananas. Their inex-
perience as consumers was touching. Then the spectacle of their
collective hunger for material goods, which showed no restraint
or discrimination, antagonized us. These people weren't worthy
of the pure and abstract freedom we had devised for them. The
sense of affliction we'd been accustomed to feeling about those
who lived "under the Communist yoke" gradually turned into a
disapproving observation of the use they made of their freedom.
We liked them better when they were lining up for sausage and
books, deprived of everything, so we could savor the luck and
superiority of belonging to the "free world."

The hazy lack of differentiation in the world "behind the iron curtain" cleared to reveal two distinct nations. The Germany of which Mauriac had said "I love it so much, I'm glad there are two" was reunified. The rumor was going around that politics was dead. The advent of a "new world order" was declared. The end of History was nigh, Democracy would cover the earth. Never had we believed with such conviction that the world was headed in a new direction. In the middle of a heat wave, the indolent order of vacation time was shattered. The enormous headline SADDAM HUSSEIN INVADES KUWAIT recalled another of the same date, fifty-one years earlier, often reproduced, GERMANY INVADES POLAND. Within days, Western powers mobilized in support of the United States. France flaunted the *Clemenceau** and considered a call to arms, as at the time of Algeria. Beyond all doubt, World War III was imminent if Saddam Hussein didn't pull out of Kuwait.

There was a need for war, as if people had suffered a lack of events for a long time, coveting the ones they could only experience as television viewers. There was a desire to reconnect with age-old tragedy. By grace of the drabbest of all American presidents, troops would be dispatched to fight "the new Hitler." Pacifists were sent to Munich. Under the spell of media simplifications, people believed in the technological delicacy of bombs, "clean war," "smart weapons," and "surgical strikes": "a civilized war," wrote *Libération*. People let out their breath in a belligerent and virtuous sigh of relief. "Kicking Saddam's ass" was a *just* war, a "lawfare," and though no one said so, a legiti-

---

* Aircraft carrier; with her sister ship the *Foch*, the mainstay of the French fleet.

mate opportunity to be finished, for once and for all, with the complicated Arab world, whose children in the *banlieue* and veiled daughters occasionally got on our nerves, but who, at the moment, as luck would have it, were staying out of trouble.

We who had broken with Mitterrand when he appeared on the screen and tonelessly declared "Guns will talk," and who couldn't bear the spirited propaganda for "Desert Storm," had only the puppet newsreaders from *Les Guignols de l'info* to raise our spirits in the evening, and *Big Bertha* once a week. In that cold and foggy January, streets were deserted, cinemas and theaters empty.

Saddam promised a mysterious "mother of all battles." It never came. The aims of war grew increasingly obscure. Bombs caused thousands of invisible deaths in Baghdad. The hostilities ended in a pall of shame, one Sunday in February, with routed Iraqi soldiers lost in the sand. The fracas ceased without really ending, for the "devil" Saddam Hussein was still on the loose and Iraq under embargo. There was mortification for having let ourselves be possessed, and humiliation for having devoted all our thoughts and feelings for days to a fiction wrought by CNN propaganda. We didn't want to hear another word about a "new world order."

The USSR, which we no longer thought about, shook the summer awake with a half-baked coup by old Stalinist fogies. Gorbachev was discredited, chaos declared and dismissed within hours, all because of a beady-eyed brute who, by some miracle, had clambered onto a tank and been hailed as the hero of freedom. The affair was skillfully managed, the USSR disappeared and became the Russian Federation with Boris Yeltsin as president. Leningrad was St. Petersburg again, much more convenient for finding one's way around the novels of Dostoevsky.

Women, more than ever, were a closely watched group whose behaviors, tastes, and desires were subject to assiduous discourse and uneasy, triumphant attention. They were now deemed to "have it all" and "be everywhere." Girls "did better at school than boys." As usual people looked for signs of emancipation in women's bodies, in their sexual and sartorial daring. The fact that they talked about "cruising guys," discussed their fantasies, and wondered aloud in *Elle* if they were "good in bed" was proof of their freedom and their equality with men. The perpetual display of their breasts and thighs in advertising was supposed to be construed as a tribute to feminine beauty. Feminism was a vengeful, humorless old ideology that young women no longer needed, and viewed with condescension. They did not doubt their own strength or their equality. (But they still read more novels than men, as if they needed to give their lives an imaginary shape.) "Thank you, men, for loving women," read a headline in a women's magazine. The struggle of women sank into oblivion. It was the only struggle that had not been officially revived in collective memory.

With the pill they had become the sole rulers of their lives, but word hadn't got out yet.

We, who had undergone kitchen-table abortions, who had

divorced and believed our struggle to free ourselves would be of use to others, were now overwhelmed by fatigue. We no longer knew if the women's revolution had really happened. We continued to see blood after fifty. It didn't have the same color or odor as before, it was a sort of illusory blood, but we were reassured by this regular scansion of time that could be sustained until death. We wore jeans, leggings, and T-shirts like girls of fifteen. Like them we said "my boyfriend" when referring to our regular lover. As we aged we ceased to have an age. When we heard *Only You* or *Capri c'est fini* on Radio Nostalgie, the sweetness of youth washed over us. The present swelled and carried us back to our twenties. Compared to our mothers, strained and perspiring throughout menopause, we felt as if we had outsmarted time.

(Young women dreamed of binding a man to themselves; those of over fifty, who'd had all that already, didn't want it anymore.)

Children, especially boys, had trouble leaving the family home with its well-stocked fridge, washed and folded clothes, and background hum of childhood. They made love in all innocence in the room next to ours. They settled into a protracted youth; the world wasn't waiting for them. And by continuing to feed and care about them, we lived in a time that stretched back uninterrupted to their childhood.

The photo of a woman facing the camera, visible from the thighs up. She stands in a garden filled with brush. Her long reddish-blonde hair trails in separate strands over the collar of a big black coat, loose and expensive-looking. A section of scarf, candy-pink and strangely narrow compared to the coat, is draped over the left shoulder. In her arms she holds a black-and-white cat of the most common variety. She smiles at the camera with her head slightly tilted, gently seductive. The lips appear very pink, probably enhanced with gloss to match the scarf. The part in her hair is a stripe of a lighter color, indicating regrowth. The full face and high cheekbones draw a youthful contrast with the circles under the eyes and the fine lines on the forehead. One cannot discern the body's girth in the bulky coat, but the hands and wrists that emerge from the sleeves to hold the cat are thin with prominent joints. It is a winter photo, the sunlight pale on the skin of the face and hands. Tufts of dry grass and barren branches stand out on a background of vegetation and a distant line of buildings. On the back is written, *Cergy, 3 February '92.*

She radiates a kind of contained abandon, or "fulfillment," as the magazines say of women between forty and fifty-five. The photo was taken in the garden below the house where she lives alone with the cat, a year-and-a-half-old female. Ten years before, she lived there with her husband, two teenage sons, and sometimes her mother. She was the hub of a wheel that could not turn without her, the maker of all decisions, from washing the sheets to booking hotels for the holidays. Her husband is far away now, remarried with a new child. Her mother is dead and her sons live elsewhere. Serenely she notes this dispossession as an inevitable part of her trajectory. When she shops for groceries at Auchan, she no longer needs a trolley; a basket is enough. She returns to nurturing only on weekends when her sons come home. Outside of work obligations, teaching and correcting class work, her time is devoted to personal pleasures and desires, reading, films, phone calls, correspondence, and love affairs. The incessant concern for others, material and moral, which characterized marriage and family life, has faded. It has been replaced by an interest in humanitarian causes, which is lighter. In this dissolving of constraints and opening of possibilities, she feels she is in step with the times, as they are delineated in *Elle* or *Marie Claire* for thirty-something women of the middle and upper classes.

Once in a while she looks at herself naked in the bathroom mirror. A delicate torso, small breasts, very slender waist, slightly rounded belly. The thighs are heavy, with a bulge above the knees. The sex is clearly visible, now that the hair is more sparse, the cleft small compared with the ones displayed in X-rated films. Near the groin, two blue streaks, traces of stretch marks from her pregnancies. She is surprised; it is the same body she's had since she stopped growing at around the age of sixteen.

In that moment, as she gazes softly at the lens—it is undoubtedly a man taking the photo—she sees herself as a woman who, three years before, was consumed by a violent passion for a Russian. Her state of desire and pain has disappeared, though she still feels its shape. The man's face grows increasingly distant and aggrieved. She would like to recall the way in which she thought about him after he left France, the torrent of images that washed over her and sealed his presence inside her, as if inside a tabernacle.

When it comes to her mother, she remembers the eyes, the hands, the silhouette; the voice, only in the abstract, without texture. The real voice is lost; she has no concrete remnant of it. But phrases often rise to her lips spontaneously, the same ones her mother used in the same contexts, expressions she didn't remember ever using herself, "The weather is sluggish," "He talked my ear off," "You have to wait your turn, like at confession," etc. It was if her mother were speaking through her mouth, and with her an entire lineage. Other phrases come into her head sometimes, the ones her mother used after she got Alzheimer's. Their incongruity revealed her mother's altered mental state, "You can bring me some rags to wipe my bottom with." In a flash, her mother's body and presence are returned to her. Unlike the former sentences, repeatedly used, the latter are unique, forever the preserve of one sole being in the world, her mother.

Her husband she hardly ever thinks about, though inside she bears the imprint of their life together and the tastes he imparted, for Bach and sacred music, the morning orange juice. When images of that life cross her mind—like one of an afternoon in Annecy, when she frantically searched the shops of the old quarter for the makings of Christmas Eve dinner, she was twenty-five and it was their first Christmas with the child—she asks, "Would I like to be there now?" She wants to say no, but she knows the question is meaningless, that no question related to things of the past has meaning.

As she waits at the hypermarket checkout, she occasionally thinks of all the times she's stood in line with a cart heaped with food. She sees the vague silhouettes of women, alone or with children circling their cart. They are faceless, distinguished only by hairstyle—a low chignon, hair cut short, in a bob, or loose and medium-long—and clothing—the seventies maxi-coat, the black midi-coat from the eighties. She sees them as images of herself, taken apart and separated like matryochka dolls. She pictures herself here in ten or fifteen years with a cart filled with sweets and toys for grandchildren not yet born. But she sees that woman as improbable, just as the girl of twenty-five saw the woman of forty, whom she has since become and already ceased to be.

When she can't sleep at night, she tries to remember the details of all the rooms where she has slept: the one she shared with her parents until the age of thirteen, the ones at the university residence and the Annecy apartment facing the cemetery. She starts at the door and makes her way around the walls. The objects that appear are always linked to gestures and singular facts: in her room at the summer camp where she'd worked as a counselor, the mirror over the sink where some boy counselors had written, in her red Diamond Enamel toothpaste, "Long live whores"; the blue lamp in her room in Rome that gave her an electrical shock each time she turned it on. In those rooms, she never sees herself with the clarity of photos, but blurred as in a film on an encrypted TV channel. Or she sees a silhouette, a hairstyle, movements—leaning out of a window, washing her hair—and positions—sitting at a desk or lying on a bed. Sometimes she manages to feel she is back inside her former body, not the way one is in dreams, but more as if she were inside the "glorious body" of the Catholic religion, which was supposed to resurrect after death with no sensation of pain or pleasure, heat, cold, or the urge to urinate. She doesn't know what she wants from these inventories, except maybe through the accumulation of memories of objects, to again become the person she was at such and such a time.

She would like to assemble these multiple images of herself, separate and discordant, thread them together with the story of her existence, starting with her birth during World War II up until the present day. Therefore, an existence that is singular but also merged with the movements of a generation. Each time she begins, she meets the same obstacles: how to represent the passage of historical time, the changing of things, ideas, and manners, and the private life of this woman? How to make the fresco of forty-five years coincide with the search for a self outside of History, the self of suspended moments transformed into the poems she wrote at twenty ("Solitude," etc.)? Her main concern is the choice between "I" and "she." There is something too permanent about "I," something shrunken and stifling, whereas "she" is too exterior and remote. The image she has of her book in its nonexistent form, of the impression it should leave, is the one she retained from *Gone with the Wind*, read at the age of twelve, and later from *Remembrance of Things Past*, and more recently from *Life and Fate*: an image of light and shadow streaming over faces. But she hasn't yet discovered how to do this. She awaits if not a revelation then a sign, a happenstance, as the madeleine dipped in tea was for Marcel Proust.

Even more than this book, the future is the next man who will make her dream, buy new clothes, and wait: for a letter, a phone call, a message on the answering machine.

The excitement of world events receded. The unexpected was tiring. Something intangible was sweeping us away. The space of experience lost its familiar contours. As the years accumulated, our landmarks, 1968 and 1981, were erased. The new break in time was the fall of the Wall, no need to specify the date. It didn't mark the end of History, just the end of the history that we could tell. Countries in Central and Eastern Europe—until now absent from our geographical imagination—seemed to multiply and endlessly divide into "ethnic groups," a term which distinguished them from us and other serious populations. It suggested backwardness, the proof of which was the return of religions and intolerance.

Yugoslavia was in a state of bloody mayhem. Bullets whistled back and forth across the streets from the weapons of invisible shooters, snipers. But as the shells vied to wipe out passersby, reduce thousand-year-old bridges to dust, and the formerly "new" philosophers vied to shame us, going out of their way to repeat, "Sarajevo is only two hours from Paris," we kept to ourselves, overcome with fatigue. We'd exerted too much emotion during the Gulf War, for no good reason. Conscience retracted. We were angry with the Croats, the Kosovars, etc., for killing each other like savages instead of copying us. We did not feel we belonged to the same Europe as them.

Algeria was a bloodbath. Under the masked faces of the members of GIA* we saw those of the FLN. The Algerians too had made poor use of their freedom, but a long time ago. It was as if from the time of Independence, we'd determined to stop thinking about it for once and for all. We wanted even less to concern ourselves with the events in Rwanda. We failed to distinguish between Hutus and Tutsis, couldn't remember who the good guys were and who the bad. The thought of Africa had always filled us with torpor. It was tacitly acknowledged that Africa lived in an earlier period of history, with barbarian customs and potentates who owned châteaux in France, and its sufferings never seemed to end. It was the discouraging continent.

Voting for or against Maastricht was an abstract gesture that we almost forgot to perform, despite the injunctions of a pressure group called *les personnalités* whose view of the issue was supposed to be shrewder than ours, though we couldn't see how. It had become a matter of course for celebrities to dictate what we should do and think. The Right, of course, would beat the Left in the legislative elections in March, and again cohabit with Mitterrand. He was an exhausted old man with sunken, too-bright eyes and a toneless voice, a skin-and-bones wreck

---

* Armed Islamic Group of Algeria (Groupe Islamique Armé).

of a head of state, whose admissions about his cancer and his secret daughter sealed his abandonment of politics, and obliged us to see nothing in him except, beyond his wiles and compromises, the terrible specter of the "time he had left." He found the strength to call the journalists "dogs" when his former prime minister, Bérégovoy, put a bullet in his head on the banks of the Loire. But it was well known that the little Russian hadn't killed himself over an apartment, but because he had betrayed his origins and ideals in the gilded halls of the Republic, where he had slavishly endured all manner of humiliations in order to remain.

Anomie was catching. Language was depleted of reality, its progressive abstraction considered a sign of intellectual distinction. Competitiveness, job insecurity, employability and flexibility were all the rage. We lived within sanitized discourse that we barely listened to, remote control having curtailed the running time of boredom.

The representation of society was fragmented into "subjects," primarily sexual: swingers, transsexuals, incest, pedophilia, bare breasts on beaches, for or against? People were confronted by facts and behaviors of which they generally had no personal experience but assumed to be widespread, even the norm, whether or not they approved. Confidences left the realm of anonymous readers' letters, the nighttime voices of *Allô Macha*. They entered bodies and faces, presented in close-ups we couldn't tear our eyes away from, amazed that so many dared to tell their intimate stories to thousands of viewers, and happy to learn so much about other people's lives. The dull murmur of social reality was drowned out by the euphoria of advertising, opinion polls, and stock market prices. "The economy is back on track again!"

They arrived of necessity from the Third World and the former Eastern bloc, lumped under the ominous appellation of *clandestins*,* herded into the Hôtel Arcade at Charles de Gaulle Airport, or turned back whenever possible by decree of the Pasqua laws. We had forgotten about *Touche pas à mon pote!* and "immigration, the wealth of France." Now we had to "fight unregulated immigration" and "preserve national identity." Michel Rocard's "France cannot take on all the misery of the world" was making the rounds, presented as a blindingly obvious fact whose unspeakable subtext was understood by most, i.e., there were already quite enough immigrants in France.

One of the ideas people rejected was that France had become a country of immigrants. For years they had continued to believe that the families from Sub-Saharan Africa and the Maghreb, who lived crowded together at the city limits, were just passing through and would return whence they came, along with their progeny, leaving a backwash of exoticism and regret, as in the lost colonies. But now it was understood that they were here to stay. The "third generation" resembled a new wave of immigration, this time from within. It swelled and encircled the cities, flooded suburban high schools, the National Employment Agency, the northern line of the RER, and the Champs-Élysées on December 31. It was a dangerous popula-

---

* Illegal immigrants, *sans papiers*.

tion, always ignored and always under surveillance, right down to its imagination, which annoyed us insofar as it was focused elsewhere, on Algeria and Palestine. They were officially called "youth from immigrant backgrounds," or in daily life, Arabs and Africans, or to employ a more virtuous phrasing, *les Beurs* and *les Blacks*. They were IT professionals, secretaries, and security guards. That they called themselves French we privately found absurd, a usurped claim to glory to which they were not yet entitled.

Retail spaces multiplied and expanded into open countryside, concrete rectangles bristling with plaques easily read from the highway, venues for diehard consumption where the act of buying was performed in an ambience of stark minimalism. Each Soviet-style block contained every object that existed in a given range of goods, shoes, clothing, home repair supplies, all in monstrous quantities, a McDonald's thrown in as a reward for the kids. Next door, the hypermarket unfurled its two thousand square meters of food and other merchandise, each category subdivided into a dozen brands. Shopping involved more time and complications, especially for those who only earned the minimum wage. The profusion of Western wealth was there to behold and handle in parallel aisles of goods, which stretched from the top of the center aisle as far as the eye could see. But we rarely looked up.

It was a place of swift and unparalleled shifts of emotion, curiosity, surprise, bewilderment, envy, loathing—of rapid-fire battles between impulse and reason. During the week, it was a choice destination for an afternoon walk, for retired couples an excuse for an outing and the slow filling of a cart. On Saturdays, whole families streamed in, and casually reveled in the nearness of so many objects of desire.

With pleasure or annoyance, lightness of heart or deep despondency, depending on the day, more and more, the acquisition of things (which we later said we couldn't do without), was life's magnetic north. When we listened to the latest song by Alain Souchon, *Foule sentimentale,* it was as if we'd jumped a hundred years ahead and were observing ourselves as people of the future would do. We had the melancholy feeling of being unable to change anything about whatever it was that was sweeping us away.

However, we got cold feet when it came to buying a new appliance ("I've gotten along fine so far without it"), whose instructions we'd have to read with the usual annoyance, whose handling we'd have to learn, finally caving in under the pressure of others who sang its praises, "you'll see, it'll change your life." It was the price to pay for going the way of greater freedom and happiness. The first use was daunting. Unfamiliar sensations arose and disappeared just as soon. With practice they vanished completely: the initial difficulty in hearing the voices on the answering machine, which (we learned) could be stored like objects and listened to ten times over; our bedazzled joy on seeing fresh-written words of love scroll up on a white fax page; the strange presence of absent beings, so vivid it produced a sense of delinquency when we didn't pick up the receiver and instead let the machine talk, frozen by fear of being heard if we made a noise.

People said: "In time, everyone will use the computer." But we did not intend to have one. It was the first object to which we'd ever felt inferior. We left its mastery to others, and envied them for it.

The fear of AIDS was the most powerful fear on record. The emaciated and transfigured faces of the famous dying, Hervé Guibert, Freddie Mercury (in his final video, so much more handsome than before, with his rabbit teeth), demonstrated the supernatural character of the "scourge"—the first sign of an end-of-millennium curse, a final judgment. We kept our distance from the HIV-positive, three million on the planet, whom the State, in moralistic television spots, strove to convince us not to view as lepers. The shame of AIDS replaced another, now forgotten, that of unwed pregnant girls. Even to be suspected of having AIDS was equal to condemnation, *does Isabelle Adjani have AIDS?* Just getting tested was suspect, an avowal of unspeakable misconduct. One had it done at the hospital, secretly, with a number, avoiding eye contact in the waiting room. Only those contaminated through transfusion ten years earlier were entitled to compassion. People found relief from the fear of others' blood by applauding the appearance in High Court of government ministers and a doctor charged with "poisoning." But on the whole, we adapted. We made a habit of carrying a condom in our purse. We didn't take it out. To use it seemed both futile and insulting to our partner. Immediately regretful, we went for the test and awaited the outcome, certain that we were dying. When we learned that we were not, simply to exist, to walk down the street, was an experience of indescribable beauty and richness. But one had to choose between fidelity and the condom. Just when pleasure in every possible form was mandatory, sexual freedom again became impracticable.

Teenagers listened to *Doc et Difool* on *Fun Radio*, lived immersed in sex and kept their secrets to themselves.

The unemployed population of France was equal in number to the seropositive population of the entire earth. In churches, petitions were laid at the foot of statues, "please Lord, may my dad find work." Everyone demanded an end to unemployment, that other "scourge," but no one believed it possible. It had become an irrational hope, an ideal that would never again be fulfilled in this world. The signs of "strength" (peace, economic recovery, a decrease in the number of job applicants), staged with handshakes—that of Arafat and Ehud Barak—abounded. Real or not, we were no longer interested. Nothing equaled the bliss at the end of the day, after elbowing one's way with the first passengers into the crowded RER, and inching as close as possible to the center aisle seats, and standing for three stations, of finally sitting down and closing one's eyes, or doing a crossword.

To the great relief of all, a useless occupation was found for the homeless, selling *The Streetlamp* and *The Street*, newspapers whose content was as shabby and stale as the vendors' clothing, and which one threw away without a second look. It was a sham activity that allowed one to distinguish between the good homeless, willing to work, and the others, sprawled and sleeping off an endless drunk on benches in the Métro, or outside next to their dog. In summer they migrated south. The mayors forbade them to lie down in pedestrian thoroughfares, dedicated to the orderly functioning of commerce. Several died of cold each winter and of heat each summer.

The presidential elections were approaching. We didn't expect our lives (collective or otherwise) to be disrupted. Mitterrand had exhausted all hope. The only candidate we might have liked was Jacques Delors, had he not stepped down after keeping us in suspense. It was no longer an event but an entertaining interlude, a show whose lead actors were three fairly average guys, two of them sad—strutting Balladur, balking Jospin—and a crazy agitated Chirac, as if the solemnity and seriousness of elections had gone out with Mitterrand. Later we would not so much recall the candidates and their speeches as we would their puppet twins, whom we watched each night on Canal+: Jospin a harmless yo-yo driving a little car along the winding roads of an enchanted kingdom, Chirac as Abbé Pierre in a monk's habit, Sarkozy a treacherous weasel obsequiously deep-bowing before a goitered Balladur, Robert Hue with his seventies shoulder bag, labeled a buffoon by the young, and we'd hear a hit song that made the puppets run amok in another *Guignols* sketch, *The Rhythm of the Night*. We believed in nothing, but when we guessed from the journalists' glowing faces that Chirac had been elected, and saw dapper youths and ladies from the chic districts scream for joy, we understood that the fun was over. The weather was as warm as in the middle of summer. Families lingered on the café terraces, the next day was a holiday, and one could have sworn the election had never happened.

Listening to Chirac, we had to make an effort to grasp that he was the president and lose the habit of Mitterrand. The series of years that had passed imperceptibly with him as a backdrop to an era now coagulated into a single block. We counted fourteen years. We didn't want to have aged that much. Young people didn't do the calculation, and had no feeling about it. Mitterrand was their de Gaulle. They'd grown up with him, and fourteen years was quite enough.

One Sunday in the middle of the 1990s, at the table where we'd managed to assemble the children, now approaching their thirties, and their friends and partners—not the same as those of the year before, passengers in a family circle from which they departed having only just arrived—around a leg of lamb—or any other dish that for lack of time, money, or skill, we knew they would not eat anywhere but at our home— and a Saint-Julien or Chassagne-Montrachet to educate the palate of these drinkers of Coke and beer, the past was of no consequence. Male voices dominated the conversation, whose subject was computers. They compared PCs and Macs, "memories" and "programs." We waited good-naturedly for them to abandon their off-putting lingo, which we had no desire for them to translate, and return to subjects of common exchange. They mentioned the latest cover of *Charlie Hebdo* and the most recent episodes of *The X-Files*, cited American and Japanese films, and advised us to see *Man Bites Dog* and *Reservoir Dogs*, whose opening scene they described with relish. They laughed affectionately at our musical tastes—total crap—and offered to lend us the latest Arthur H. They commented on the news with the derision of *Les Guignols*, their daily information source along with *Libération*, and refused to commiserate with individual misfortune, saying "to each his own shit." Their stance was one of ironic distancing of the world. Their lively repartee and verbal agility dazzled and mortified us. We were afraid of coming across as slow and ungainly. They renewed our supply of words commonly used by the young, astutely imparted so we too could inject "Wicked!" and "How twisted is that!" into our exchanges.

With the satisfaction of the part-time nurturer, we watched them eat and take extra helpings of everything. Later over champagne came the memories of TV shows, household products, ads and fashions from their childhood and adolescence: balaclavas, iron-on knee patches, the SaniCrush electric toilet macerator, Three Kittens brand jam biscuits, Hot Wheels, Kiri the clown, Laurel & Hardy collector stamps, etc. As the objects of their common past resurfaced, they competed with each other to produce the best quote, a vast and futile remembering that made them seem like little boys again.

The afternoon light had shifted. The waves of excitement came at longer intervals. The suggestion of a game of Scrabble, which always made them argue, was sensibly dismissed.

Immersed in the aroma of coffee and cigarettes (by tacit agreement, no cannabis was brought out), we savored the sweetness of a ritual that had weighed so heavily upon us once that we'd wanted to flee it for good. Beyond marital breakdown, the death of grandparents, and a general growing apart, we'd ensured its continuity with a white tablecloth, silverware, and a joint of meat, on this Sunday afternoon in the spring of 1995. And as we watched and listened to these grown children, we wondered what bound us to each other. It wasn't blood or genes, only a present comprised of thousands of days spent together, words and gestures, meals, car trips, a great deal of shared experience that left no conscious trace.

They kissed us four times on the cheeks and left. In the evening we recalled their pleasure in eating at our home with their friends. We were happy to continue providing for their oldest and most basic need, food. In our boundless concern for them, reinforced by the belief that we'd been stronger at their age, we perceived them as fragile beings in a shapeless future.

In the heat of late July we learned that a bomb had exploded in the Saint-Michel Métro station. Naturally, the attacks would return with Chirac. We recovered the reflex of calling the people close to us, convinced until we heard their voices that of all the places they might have been, fate had put them on that train and in that car on the RER B, at that very moment. There were dead and wounded. Someone had had their legs blown off. But the big August holiday was coming, and we had no desire to become anxious. We walked through the Métro corridors followed by a voice that enjoined us to report abandoned parcels, putting our fate at the mercy of the safety measures.

A few weeks later, after we had forgotten about Saint-Michel, came other bombings involving a curious mixture of pressure cookers, nails, and gas cylinders. As if watching a film we followed the hunt for "the mysterious Kelkal," a young man from the suburbs of Lyon, and saw him die, shot down by police before he could utter a word. It was the first year that daylight saving time was prolonged until the end of October, an autumn of heat and light. Other than the families of the victims and survivors, who remembered the dead of Saint-Michel Métro? Their names appeared nowhere, probably so as not to frighten Métro patrons, already so unnerved by delays due to "technical incidents" or "serious accidents involving a passenger." These deaths were more quickly forgotten than those of rue de Rennes, though the latter had occurred nine years earlier, and those of rue des Rosiers, even more distant. The facts slipped away before one even got around to telling the story.

Dispassion grew.

The world of commodities and commercials and that of political speeches coexisted on television but did not coincide. One was ruled by ease and the call to pleasure, the other by sacrifice and constraint, with phrases that grew increasingly

ominous: "the globalization of trade," "necessary moderniza-
tion." It had taken us a while to translate the Juppé Plan into
images of daily life and to understand we were being screwed.
But we were tired of that haughty and condescending way
of reproaching us for not being "pragmatic." Retirement and
social security were the State's last show of concern, a kind of
anchor point amidst all the things being swept away.

Railway and postal employees stopped working, as did
teachers and all public employees. Paris and other large cities
were riddled with inescapable traffic jams. People bought bicycles to get around and walked in hurried columns through the
December night. It was a winter strike, an adult strike, somber
and unruffled, with neither violence nor exaltation. We redis-
covered the disjointed temporality of major strikes. Delay was
the order of the day, along with resourcefulness and provisional
organization. There was myth in people's bodies and gestures.
The indefatigable walking through the streets of a Paris devoid
of subways and buses was an act of memory. The voice of Pierre
Bourdieu at the Gare de Lyon united '68 to '95. We believed
again. Calmly we were galvanized by new phrases like "another
world," and "creating a social Europe." People kept remarking
that they hadn't spoken to each other in this way for years. We
marveled. The strike was more word than action. Juppé withdrew his plan. Christmas was on its way. We had to return to
ourselves, to gifts and patience. Those December days drew to
a close and told no story. All that remained was the image of
a crowd trudging through darkness. We didn't know if it was
the last major strike of the century or a new awakening. For
us, something was beginning. Éluard came to our minds: *There*

were only a few of them / In all the earth / Each one thought he was alone / . . . They were suddenly a crowd.

Between what is yet to come and what is, consciousness is empty for a moment. We gazed uncomprehending at the huge front-page headline in *Le Monde*, FRANÇOIS MITTERRAND IS DEAD. As in December, crowds gathered in darkness at Place de la Bastille. We continued to need to be together and what we felt was solitude. We recalled that on the evening of May 10, 1981, in the town hall of Château-Chinon, Mitterrand, learning he had been elected president of the Republic, had murmured "How about that!"

Our emotions were raw. Waves of fear, indignation, and joy ruffled the even surface of days that otherwise lacked surprise. We no longer ate beef because of "mad cow disease," which would cause the death of thousands in the coming decade. We were shocked by the image of an ax smashing down on the door of a church where a group of *sans papiers* had taken refuge. A sudden sense of inequity, a blaze of feeling or conscience drove hordes of people into the streets. One hundred thousand joyously marched in protest of the Debré bill, which facilitated the expulsion of foreigners. They pinned a button on their backpacks, the image of a black suitcase and the slogan *Who's next?* They tucked it in a drawer at home as a memento. They signed petitions and forgot the cause, forgot they'd even signed them—who was Abu-Jamal, again? Then, overnight, their energy flagged. Effusion alternated with anomie, protest with consent. The word "struggle" was discredited as a throwback to Marxism, become an object of ridicule. As for "defending rights," the first that came to mind were those of the consumer.

Some sentiments fell out of use, ones we no longer felt and found absurd, such as patriotism and honor, reserved for inferior times and abused populations. Shame, invoked at every turn, was a shadow of its former self—a passing aggravation, a short-lived wound to the ego. "Respect," first and foremost, was the demand of that same ego for the recognition of others. One no longer heard the words "goodness" or "good people." Pride in what one did was substituted for pride in what one was—female, gay, provincial, Jewish, Arab, etc.

The feeling most encouraged was a confused sense of dangerousness associated with the pixelated face of the "Romanian"—the "savage" of the *banlieue*, purse snatcher, rapist, pedophile, swarthy terrorist—and with Métro corridors, the Gare du Nord, the neighborhood of Seine-Saint-Denis. Reinforced by programs on TF1 and M6, and by public-address announcements ("Beware of pickpockets in this station," "Report all unattended packages"), it was the feeling of being unsafe.

There was no specific word for the feeling one had of simultaneous stagnation and mutation. In the general failure to grasp what was happening, a word began making the rounds, "values" (no one specified which), for example, the sweeping condemnation of youth, education, pornography, the PACS bill,* cannabis, and the deterioration of spelling. Others jeered at this "new moral order," the "politically correct" and "prefab thinking." They commended transgression and applauded the cynicism of Michel Houellebecq. On television, languages collided without fracas.

We were inundated with explanations of self, tirelessly supplied by Mireille Dumas, Delarue, women's magazines, and *Psychologies*. They didn't teach us much of anything but gave us permission to hold our parents to account, and the consolation of merging our experience with that of others.

Thanks to Chirac's entertaining whim of dissolving the Assembly, the Left won the elections and Jospin became prime minister. It made up for the evening of disappointment in May 1995, reinstated the lesser evil along with measures that had a tang of freedom, equality, and generosity. This was compatible with our desire to be entitled, one and all, to the good things in life: universal health insurance and time to ourselves with the thirty-five-hour workweek, even if the rest remained unchanged. And we would not spend the year 2000 under the Right.

The order of the market closed in and imposed its breakneck pace. Goods marked with bar codes slipped more quickly than ever from conveyor belt to shopping cart. A discreet beep conjured away the transaction's cost in an instant. Back-to-school supplies

---

* *Pacte civil de solidarité*, civil solidarity pact, a contractual form of civil union between two adults. Voted in 1999, primarily to offer some legal status to same-sex couples.

filled the shelves before children had started their summer holidays, Christmas toys appeared on the shelves the day after All Saints' Day, swimsuits in February. The timing of things pulled us into its vortex and forced us to live two months ahead of ourselves. People flocked to "special openings" on Sundays or evenings until eleven. The first day of sales was a media event. "Getting a deal," and "saving big" were part of an undisputed principle, an obligation. The shopping center, with its hypermarket and arcades, became our chief habitat, a place for the tireless contemplation of objects and quiet pleasures, violence-free, protected by security guards with bulging muscles. Grandparents took the kids to see the goats and chickens in odor-free litter under artificial lighting, replaced the next day by specialties from Brittany or mass-produced necklaces and statues, marketed as African art, all that remained of colonial history. Teenagers, especially those who could rely on no other means of social distinction, acquired personal value through brands, *L'Oréal—because I'm worth it.* And we, high and mighty despisers of consumer society, yielded to the yearning for a pair of boots which, like the long-ago sunglasses, miniskirt, and bell-bottoms, created a brief illusion of renewal. More than a sense of possession it was this feeling people sought on the shelves of Zara and H&M, instantly granted upon acquiring a thing, a little shot of extra being.

And we did not age. The things around us didn't last long enough to grow old, replaced and rehabilitated at lightning speed. Our memory didn't have time to associate them with moments of existence.

Of all the new objects the "mobile phone" was the most miraculous and disturbing. Never had we imagined being able one day to walk down the street with a phone in our pocket and call anyone, anywhere, at any time. It was strange to see people talking to themselves on the street, a phone pressed to one ear. The first time we heard the ringing in our purse on the RER, or at the checkout, we gave a start and feverishly searched the OK button with a kind of shame, of malaise. Our body suddenly drew attention to itself as we said hello, yes, and words not intended for the ears of strangers. Conversely, when a voice piped up beside us to answer a call, we were irritated, captives of a life that obviously held ours to be nonexistent and thrust its insipid dailiness upon us, the banality of worries and desires which until then had been consigned to phone booths or apartments.

The real test of technological courage was to use the computer. Those who were able enjoyed superior access to modernity and a new and different form of intelligence. It was a domineering object that required quick reflexes and exceptionally precise movements of the hands. In unfathomable English, it continually suggested "options," which had to be obeyed without a moment's delay. Pitiless and evil, it concealed in its inmost depths the letter we'd just composed. It cast us into constant ruin and humiliation, drove us to revolt, "what's it done to me now!" Our dismay forgotten, we bought a modem so we could have Internet access and an email address, dazzled by our "navigation" of the entire world on AltaVista.

There was something about these new objects that was hard on body and mind, but it quickly disappeared with use. They grew light. (As usual children and teenagers used the computer with ease and without questions.)

The typewriter, with its rattle and accessories, the eraser, stencil, and carbon paper seemed to us to belong to a distant, unthinkable time. Yet when we pictured ourselves, a few years earlier, calling X from a pay phone in a café restroom, or typing a letter to P at night on an Olivetti, it was obvious that the absence of a mobile phone and email had no place in either the joys or sufferings of life.

On a background of pale blue sky and a near-deserted sand beach with furrows like a plowed field, two women and two men stand in a tight little group. The four faces are pressed close to each other, each divided into zones of darkness and light by the sun, which slants down from the left. The two men are in the middle. They look alike—thirtyish, same height and build, same three- or four-day stubble. One has a receding hairline; the other's baldness is more advanced. The man on the right has his hands on the shoulders of a petite young woman with black hair framing her eyes and round cheeks. The other woman, on the far left, is of indeterminate middle age, with lines on her forehead, touched by the light, pink blush on her cheekbones and a softening facial contour. Her hair is cut in a bob. She wears pearl earrings, a beige sweater with a loosely knotted scarf, and carries a shoulder bag. All suggest a well-off city woman on a weekend visit to the Normandy coast.

She has the gentle distant smile of parents or teachers accustomed to having their picture taken with young people (a way of showing that one is quite aware of the generation gap).

All four stand facing the camera. Their bodies and faces are locked in a position that hails from the dawn of photography, attesting that they were together in the same place on the same day, with minds similarly vacant except for a sense of well-being. On the back of the photo, *Trouville, March 1999*.

She is the woman wearing blush. The men in their thirties are her sons. The young black-haired woman is the girlfriend of the older boy. The younger son's girlfriend is taking the picture. For some years the woman has enjoyed the comfortable income of a teacher with seniority and has treated them all to this weekend at the seaside. She continues to contribute to her children's material welfare to compensate for any pain they may endure in their lives, for which she feels responsible, having brought them into the world. She has decided they should enjoy life in spite of the short-term contracts for which they are overqualified, unemployment insurance or freelance work, depending on the month. Their lives are a pure present of music, American TV series, and video games, as if they continued to live as students, or impecunious artists in an old-style bohemian existence, so far removed from the settled life that had been hers at their age. (She does not know if their social nonchalance is real or feigned.)

They walked to Roches Noires and the staircase named after Marguerite Duras, then back again. In the vague, contemplative slowness of a group stroll, the disorderly and choppy adjustment of steps, perhaps she felt a kind of disbelief, gazing at the backs and legs of her sons, who walked ahead with their partners, and listening to their deep voices. How could these men be her children? That she had carried them in her womb did not seem to her enough of an explanation. Hadn't she obscurely sought to recreate her parents' twofold existence, to have ahead of her what she had behind, enjoy the same kind of anchoring in the world? And on this beach, she may have recalled the way her mother always exclaimed "Such big lads!" as she watched her approach between her teenage sons; exclaimed with admiration and amazement, as if it defied belief that her daughter could be the mother of two strapping boys, already a head taller than she, and almost improper that two males instead of two girls had grown in the body of the one who was and would always be her little girl.

Certainly, as at other times with her sons, when she takes on the mothering role she assumes only occasionally, she feels the limitations of the maternal bond, her need to have a lover, a kind of intimacy that only the sex act can provide, which also consoles her in times of passing conflict with her sons. The young man she sees on other weekends often bores her. He gets on her nerves by watching *Téléfoot* on Sunday mornings.

But if she gave him up, she would cease to communicate the insignificant acts and incidents of her day. She would no longer put daily life into words. She would stop waiting. She'd gaze at the lace stockings and thongs in the chest of drawers and tell herself she'd never wear them again. And when she heard *Sea, Sex and Sun,* she'd feel cast out of an entire world of caresses, desire, and fatigue, bereft of a future. At that moment, just to imagine it, the sense of deprivation violently attaches her to the boy as to a "last love."

She knows the main element of their relationship is not sexual, not as far as she's concerned. Through the boy she can relive something she thought she would never experience again. When he takes her to eat at Jumbo, or greets her with The Doors and they make love on a mattress on the floor of his icy studio flat, she feels she is replaying scenes from her student life, reproducing moments that have already occurred. Not living them for real now, and yet the repetition gives reality to her youth, to the first experiences, "first times" which due to their sudden irruption into her life and her own state of stupor, made no sense then. They don't make sense now either, but repetition fills the void and creates the illusion of completion. In her diary she writes: "He wrenches me away from my generation. But I am not part of his. I'm nowhere in time. He's the angel who brings the past back to life, who immortalizes."

Often as she lies against him in the half-sleep that follows love on Sunday afternoons, she lapses into a state that is like no other. She no longer knows what city or town the noises are coming from—the sounds of cars, footsteps, and words from the outside world. All at once she's in her cubicle at the girls' dormitory, and in hotel rooms (Spain in 1980, Lille with P in the winter), and in bed as a child, nestled against her sleeping mother. She feels herself in several different moments of her life that float on top of each other. Time of an unknown nature takes hold of her consciousness and her body too. It is a time in which past and present overlap, without bleeding into each other, and where, it seems, she flickers in and out of all the shapes of being she has been. It is a sensation she's had before, from time to time. Perhaps drugs could bring it on, but she has never taken any, for she values pleasure and lucidity above all else. Now, in a state of expansion and deceleration, she takes hold of the sensation. She has given it a name, "the palimp-sest sensation," though the word is not quite accurate if she relies on the dictionary meaning, "a manuscript on which the original writing has been scratched out to make room for later writing." She sees it as a potential instrument of knowledge that is not only for herself, but general, almost scientific, though a knowledge of what, she doesn't know. In her writing project about a woman who has lived between 1940 and today, which grips her ever more tightly with sorrow and even guilt for not committing it to paper, she would like to begin with this sensa-tion, no doubt influenced by Proust, out of a need to base her undertaking on a real experience.

It is a sensation that pulls her inexorably and by degrees away from words and all language, back to her first years, bereft of memory, the rosy warmth of the cradle, through a series of *abymes*—those of *Birthday*, the painting by Dorothea Tan-ning—that eliminate all her actions, all events, everything that she has learned, thought, and desired, and which has brought her over the years to be here, in this bed, with this young man. It is a sensation that cancels out her history, whereas in her book she would like to save everything that has continually been around her. She wants to save her *circumstance*. And is the sensation itself not a product of history, of such great changes in the lives of women and men that one can feel it at the age of nearly fifty-eight, lying beside a man of twenty-nine, with no sense of wrongdoing, or indeed of pride? She is not sure the "palimpsest sensation" has a more heuristic power than another sensation, also frequent, whereby her "selves" are characters in books and films and she is the woman in *Sue Lost in Manhattan* and *Claire Dolan*, which she saw not long ago, or Jane Eyre, Molly Bloom—or Dalida.

Next year she will retire. She is already deleting files and notes on books, getting rid of reference works she once used to write her courses. She peels away the former "packaging" of her life, as if to clear the boards for her writing project, which she no longer has any excuse to postpone. While going through her papers she happens on a phrase from the beginning of *The Life of Henry Brulard*: "I am going to be fifty years old. It is more than time for me to know myself." When she copied it down, she'd been thirty-seven. Now she has caught up to and surpassed the age of Stendhal.

The year 2000 was on the horizon. We could not believe our luck in being there to see it arrive. What a shame, we thought, when someone died in the weeks before. We couldn't imagine that it could proceed without a hitch. There were rumors of a Y2K computer bug, a planetary malfunction, some kind of black hole portending the end of the world and a return to the savagery of instinct. The twentieth century closed behind us in a pitiless succession of end-of-millennium reviews. Everything was listed, classified, and assessed, from works of art and literature to wars and ideologies, as if the twenty-first century could only be entered with our memories wiped clean. It was a solemn and accusatory time (we had everything to answer for). It hung darkly overhead and removed personal memories of what for us had never been an entity called "the century" but only a slipping-by of years that stood out (or didn't) depending on the changes they had brought to our lives. In the coming century, parents, grandparents, and people we'd known in childhood who had died would be dead for good.

The 1990s just past held no particular meaning for us. They'd been years of disillusionment. We had witnessed the events in Iraq—which the United States was starving out and threatening with airstrikes, where children were dying for lack of medicine—and in Gaza, the West Bank, Chechnya, Kosovo, Algeria, etc. We preferred not to remember the handshake between Arafat and Clinton at Camp David, the "new world order" that had been foretold, or Yeltsin on his tank. We preferred not to remember much of anything at all, except perhaps the foggy distant evenings of December of '95, probably the last general strike of the century. And perhaps the beautiful unhappy princess, killed in a speeding car under the Pont de l'Alma, and Monica Lewinsky's blue dress stained with Bill Clinton's semen. But we did want to remember the World Cup. It was said that people would have willingly relived the weeks of waiting around TV sets in the silent cities where pizza Mobylettes buzzed back and forth; the weeks that led match by match to that Sunday and that moment when, amidst the clamor and ecstasy we knew that, having won, we could all die happy, die together (except that it was the exact opposite of death), rediscover the great surrender to one sole desire, one image, one story. Those were dazzling days, whose derisory remains fluttered for months from the walls of the Métro: posters of Zidane for Eau d'Évian and Leader Price budget grocery.

Nothing lay ahead.

The last summer arrived—and now everything was "the last." People gathered once more. They sped away to the cliffs above the Channel, or flocked to public gardens in Paris to see the moon blot out the sun at noon. A chill descended, a kind of dusk. We were anxious for the sun's return but also yearned to linger in that peculiar darkness, the sensation of living through the extinction of humanity in fast-forward. Millions of cosmic years passed before our eyes, shrouded in dark glasses. Blind faces raised to the sky seemed to await the coming of a god or the pale rider of the Apocalypse. The sun reappeared and people clapped. There wouldn't be another solar eclipse until 2081, and we would be long gone.

And then it arrived, 2000. Apart from fireworks and a predictable urban euphoria, nothing had transpired of note. We were disappointed: the computer bug was all a scam. Then six days after the change of millennium "the big storm," as it was soon called, blew up out of nowhere. In a matter of hours that night it leveled thousands of pylons, razed forests, and tore away roofs as it gusted north to south, and west to east, having the decency to kill only a dozen or so people in the wrong place at the wrong time. The morning sun calmly rose above a savaged landscape with a beauty peculiar to ruin. So began the third millennium. (The idea of a mysterious act of revenge on the part of Nature did not fail to cross our minds.)

Nothing changed except the unfamiliar 2 instead of the 1 that continued to slide off our pen when we dated a check. With another mild and rainy winter, like the ones of the years before, the reminder of Brussels' "European directives," and the "start-up boom," a kind of melancholy prevailed instead of the expected enthusiasm. The Socialists governed in a nondescript way. There were fewer demonstrations and we no longer went to the ones in support of the *sans papiers*.

A few months after the turn of the century, the plane of the rich, which no one we knew ever took, crashed in Gonesse and swiftly vanished from memory, joining the era of de Gaulle. An icy little man of fathomless ambition, with a name that for once was easy to pronounce, Putin, had replaced the drunken Yeltsin and swore to hunt down Chechens and "bump them off, even on the crapper." Now Russia evoked neither hope nor fear, only perpetual desolation. It had withdrawn from our imaginations, which in spite of ourselves were occupied by the United States, a gigantic tree spreading its branches over the face of the earth. We were increasingly irritated by the Americans' moral discourse, their shareholders, retirement funds, pollution of the planet, and loathing for our cheeses. To signify the fundamental poverty of their superiority, based on weapons and the economy, the word typically used to define them was "arrogance." They were conquerors with no ideals other than oil and the almighty dollar. Their values and principles—don't rely on anyone but yourself—gave hope to no one but them, while we dreamed of "another world."

At first sight, it defied belief, as a film clip would later show: George W. Bush displaying no reaction, like a lost child, as the news was whispered in his ear. It could not be thought or felt but only watched, over and over, on the television screen, the Twin Towers collapsing, one after the other, that September afternoon, which was morning in New York but would always be afternoon for us. As if viewing and reviewing the images would make it real. In a state of inert horror that we were unable to shake, we watched by mobile phone, with as many people as possible.

Speeches and analyses poured in. The raw event dissipated. We bridled at *Le Monde*'s proclamation, "We are all Americans." Our image of the world was turned on its head. Some fanatical individuals from obscurantist countries, armed only with box cutters, had razed the symbols of American power in a matter of two hours. The ingenuity astounded. We berated ourselves for having believed the U.S. invincible. Revenge had been taken on an illusion. We recalled another September 11 and the assassination of Allende. Something was being paid for. Later, it would be time to exercise compassion and think of the consequences, but now all that mattered was to say when, how, and from what or whom we'd learned about the attack on the Twin Towers. The very few people who hadn't known the same day were dogged by a feeling of having missed a rendezvous with the whole world.

And everyone racked their brains for what they'd been doing at the exact moment when the first plane hit the World Trade Center and couples hurled themselves from windows hand-in-hand. There was no connection but the fact of being alive at the same moment as the three thousand human beings who were going to die, but hadn't known it fifteen minutes earlier. As we recalled "I was at the dentist, driving, at home reading," stunned by this contemporaneity, we grapsed the separation between people on earth and our bonding in a common uncertainty. As we gazed at a Van Gogh painting at the Musée d'Orsay, our ignorance of what was happening at the same second in Manhattan was identical to that of the moment when we ourselves would die. However, in the meaningless flow of days, the hour that contained the shattered towers of the World Trade Center and a dentist appointment or a car inspection was saved.

September 11 suppressed all the dates that had stayed with us until then. As they had once said "after Auschwitz," people said "after September 11," a unique day. There began we didn't know what. Time too was becoming globalized.

Later, when we think of events that, after a moment's hesitation, we'll place in 2001—a storm in Paris on the August 15 weekend, a massacre at the Cergy-Pontoise Savings Bank, *Loft Story*, the publication of *The Sexual Life of Catherine M*— we will be surprised to realize they occurred before September 11 and that nothing distinguished them from ones that happened after, in October or November. Events, facts returned to floating in the past, unmoored from an event which, we now had to admit, we hadn't actually experienced.

Before we had time to think, fear took hold of us. A dark force had infiltrated the world, prepared to commit the most atrocious acts in every corner of the planet. Envelopes filled with white powder killed their recipients. A headline in *Le Monde* referred to "the coming war." The president of the United States, George W. Bush, insipid son of the one before, ludicrously elected after endless vote recounts, proclaimed the clash of civilizations, Good against Evil. Terrorism had a name, Al Qaeda; a religion, Islam; a country, Afghanistan. The time for sleep was past. We had to be on the alert until the end of time. We were obliged to shoulder American fear, which cooled our solidarity and compassion. We poked fun at their failure to catch bin Laden and Mullah Omar, who had ridden away on a motorcycle and vanished into thin air.

Our image of the Muslim world did an about-face. This complex web of robed men, women veiled like holy virgins, camel drivers, belly dancers, minarets and muezzins, was transformed from the state of distant object, variegated, picturesque and backward, to that of a modern power. People struggled to make the connection between modernity and the pilgrimage to Mecca, a young woman wearing a chador and doing a PhD at the University of Tehran. The Muslims could no longer be forgotten. One billion two hundred million.

(The one billion three hundred million Chinese, who believed in nothing but in the economy, and churned out low-end products to sell to the West, were only a distant silence.)

Religion was making a comeback but it wasn't our religion, the one in which we no longer believed and hadn't wanted to impart, though it basically remained the only legitimate faith— the best, if one had to give it a rank. The one whose decade of the Rosary, canticles, and fish on Friday loomed large in the museum of childhood, *I am a Christian, that is my glory.*

The distinction between "dyed-in-the-wool French" and "those of immigrant background" never wavered. When in speeches the president of the Republic evoked "the people of France," he referred (it went without saying) to a generous entity, beyond all suspicion of xenophobia, of which Victor Hugo was part and parcel, along with the storming of the Bastille, country folk, schoolmasters and schoolmistresses, and priests, Abbé Pierre and de Gaulle, Bernard Pivot, Asterix, Mother Denis and Coluche, the Maries and Patricks. It didn't include Fatima, Ali, and Boubacar, the people who shopped in the halal section of hypermarkets and observed Ramadan. Even less did it include the youth from the "sensitive" neighborhoods, with hoodies that flopped down over their faces, and an apathetic gait, sure signs of cunning and laziness, of being "up to no good." In some obscure way, they were the natives of an inner colony we no longer controlled.

Language steadfastly built a partition between us and them. It confined them to "communities" in the "'hoods," "lawless enclaves" given over to drug trafficking and gang rape, and turned them into savages. *The French are worried*, journalists asserted. According to opinion polls, which dictated public emotion, lack of safety was what worried people the most. This form of menace—not that anyone said so—had the swarthy face of a shadow population, a horde quick to relieve honest people of their mobile phones.

The switch to the euro was a brief distraction. The novelty of checking the new coins' country of issue faded within a week. It was a cold currency, with clean little banknotes devoid of image or metaphor. A euro was a euro and nothing else, a barely real, weightless, and misleading currency that shrank prices, created an impression of universal economy in stores and one of increasing poverty on pay slips. It was so strange to imagine Spain without pesetas next to the tapas and sangria, or Italy without a hundred thousand lire per night for a hotel room. There was no time for the melancholy of passing things. Pierre Bourdieu, the little-known intellectual and critic, had died and we hadn't even known that he was ill. He'd given us no time to foresee his absence. A strange, quiet grief afflicted those who had felt liberated by reading his books. We were afraid that his words within us would be erased, like those of Sartre so long ago. Afraid of letting the world of opinions get the better of us.

The presidential election in May was all the more disheartening. A repeat of the previous one, in 1995, with Chirac and Jospin (the latter, Tony Blair-style, shrank from using the word "socialist" but would probably be elected). We remembered with amazement the tension and bitterness of the first months of 1981. So at least in memory we were going somewhere. Even 1995 seemed preferable. We didn't quite know what was wearing us down the most, the media and their opinion polls, *who do you trust*, their condescending comments, the politicians with their promises to reduce unemployment and plug the hole in the social security budget, or the escalator at the RER station that was always out of order, the lines at Carrefour and La Poste, the Romanian beggars, all those things that made it as futile to put a ballot in a ballot box as a contest entry form into a drum at the mall. And the *Guignols* on Canal+ weren't funny. Since no one represented us, it was only fitting that we do as we pleased, so that voting became a private, emotional affair, governed by last-minute impulse—Arlette Laguiller, or Christiane Taubira, or maybe the Greens? One needed the habit and long-standing memory of "electoral duty" to bother to go to the polling station on an April Sunday in the middle of spring vacation.

But as it turned out, the day was bright and sunny and the weather mild. Oddly, we retained no memory of all we did on that April Sunday, or of the hours before the results were announced, except perhaps for the anticipation of an evening's entertainment. And so it happened, the Sayer of anti-Semitic and racist horrors for the past twenty years, the demagogue with his rictus of hatred who played to the gallery, quietly rose and annihilated Jospin. No more Left. The political lightness of life vanished. Where had we gone wrong? What had we done? Should we not have voted for Jospin instead of Laguiller or the Greens? Conscience floundered, caught in the gap between the innocent gesture of putting the ballot in the box and the collective result. We had gone to the ends of our desire and were being punished. It was a guilty event. The discourse of shame was in full swing, and replaced the one about lack of safety, which had been going strong just the day before. The search for someone to blame quickly spun out of control. In a loop, the TV news ran images of pathetic Grandpa Voise, mauled by thugs who had also torched his miserable hovel, of abstainers and people who had voted environmentalist, Trotskyist, Communist. The media "gave the floor" to those who had silently voted for Le Pen, laborers and cashiers who emerged from the shadows and were carefully questioned for the sake of our immediate and futile comprehension.

Before we had time to think, we were swept into the frenzy of a mass mobilization to save democracy. The summons to vote for Chirac was combined with tips for keeping your soul clean while sliding the ballot into the box: hold your nose and put on gloves, *better a vote that stinks than a vote that kills*. A virtuous and browbeaten unanimity drove us docile into the crowds of May 1 and the slogans *Heil the Führer Le Pen, Don't be afraid, put up Resistance, I've got the balls J'ai les boules Tengo las bolas, 17.3% on the Hitler scale*. Young people who had just returned from the mid-term holiday said it reminded them of the World Cup. Under the gray sky of a teeming Place de la République, at the end of a huge and tight-packed procession that simply would not get moving, we were overcome by doubt. We felt like extras in a film about the thirties. There was a consensual falsity in the air. We became resigned to voting for Chirac instead of staying home. When we came out of the polling station, we felt as if we had committed a completely mindless act. That night on TV, when we saw the swell of faces raised toward Chirac crying *Chichi we love you*, while the small slender hand of SOS Racisme fluttered over the heads of the crowd, we thought *those assholes*.

Later all that we would recall of the election was the month and day of the first round, April 21, as if the forced second round with an 80 percent turnout didn't count. Was voting still possible?

We watched the Right retake all the seats. The same speeches that summoned us to adapt to the market and globalization, the same injunctions to work more and longer, blossomed anew in the mouth of a prime minister whose name, Raffarin, stooped posture, and weary affability made one think of a heavy-treaded fifties notary pacing in his office, making the floorboards creak. We were hardly even outraged to hear him speak of "the France from above" and "the France from below," as in the nineteenth century. We turned away. Even the Bleus were beaten in the World Cup in Korea. We came around again.

The August sun warmed the skin. On the sand with eyelids closed, we were the same woman, the same man. We basked in our bodies, the same we'd had in childhood on the pebble beach in Normandy and on long-ago holidays on the Costa Brava. Resurrected one more time in a shroud of light.

We opened our eyes and saw a woman walk into the sea, fully dressed in a jacket, long skirt, and a Muslim headscarf over her hair. A bare-chested man in shorts held her by the hand. It was a biblical vision whose beauty made us horribly sad.

The places where merchandise was displayed were increasingly spacious, attractive, colorful, and spotlessly clean in contrast with the bleakness of subway stations, La Poste, and public high schools. They were reborn each morning with the splendor and abundance of the first day in Eden.

Sampling at the rate of one small container a day, an entire year would not have been enough to try every available flavor of yogurt and dairy dessert. There were designated depilatory products for male and female armpits, mini-pads for G-strings, wet wipes, "creative menus" and "roasted mini-snacks" for cats, grouped into categories for kittens, adult, senior, or indoor cats. No part of the human body or its functions was spared the providence of industry. Foods were "light," or "enriched" by invisible substances, vitamins, omega-3s, and fiber. Everything in existence, air, heat, cold, grass, ants, sweat, and snoring, generated merchandise and products for the upkeep of the latter, ad infinitum, in an unrelenting subdivision of reality and proliferation of objects. The commercial imagination knew no bounds. It co-opted for its own gain all the specialty languages, ecological, psychological, etc. It draped itself in humanism and social justice, enjoined us to "fight the cost of living," issued prescriptions such as "Spoil yourself" and "Get yourself a sweet deal." It orchestrated the celebration of traditional holidays, Christmas and Valentine's Day, and accompanied Ramadan. It was a kind of ethic, a philosophy, the undisputed shape of our lives. *Life. The real thing. Auchan.*[*]

It was a sweet and happy dictatorship that no one contested. One needed only protect oneself from its excesses, educate the consumer (the primary definition of the individual). For everyone, including illegal immigrants crammed into boats off the Spanish coast, the shopping center wore the face of freedom, along with the hypermarket crumbling beneath its mountains of merchandise. It was normal for goods to arrive from all over the world and freely circulate, while men and women were turned away at the borders. To cross them, some had themselves locked into trucks, inert merchandise, and died asphyxiated when the driver forgot them in a Dover parking lot under the June sun.

The solicitude of mass-market retailers went so far as to provide a section for the poor: low-end, bulk, and no-name goods, corned beef and liverwurst that reminded the well-to-do of the shortages and austerity of the former Eastern bloc.

So the events foretold in the seventies by Debord and Dumont (wasn't there also a novel by Le Clézio?) had come

---

* A chain of hypermarkets.

to be. How could we have let it happen? But the predictions had not all become reality. We were not covered in pimples. Our skin wasn't slaking off as in Hiroshima. We didn't need to wear gas masks in the street. No, we were healthier and more attractive. To die of an illness was less and less conceivable. We could let the second millennium march on without undue worry.

We remembered our parents' reproach, "Look at all you have and you're still not happy!" Now we knew that all we had didn't add up to happiness, but that was no reason to abandon *things*. And if certain people were denied, or excluded, that was the price to be paid, it seemed, a requisite quota of lives sacrificed so the majority could reap the benefits of things.

There was an ad that read: *Money, sex, drugs—choose money.*

We graduated to the DVD player, the digital camera, the MP3 player, ADSL, and the flat screen. We never ceased to upgrade. The failure to do so meant saying yes to aging. Gradually, as the skin started to show its years and the body to feel the effects of time, the world showered us with new things. We in our decline and the world, marching on, were going in opposite directions.

The questions that arose with the appearance of new technologies were canceled out as their use became second nature, and required no thought. People who didn't know how to use a computer or a Discman would become obsolete, like those who couldn't use a phone or washing machine.

In nursing homes, an endless parade of commercials filed by the faded eyes of elderly women, for products and devices they never imagined they would need and had no chance of ever possessing.

We were snowed under by the timing of things. A balance we'd long maintained was upset, between waiting and having, privation and acquisition. Novelty no longer prompted diatribes or enthusiasm, ceased to haunt the imagination. It was our normal environment. Perhaps the very concept of "new" would vanish as the idea of progress had, or almost—such was our fate. We began to see unlimited possibilities in everything. Hearts, livers, kidneys, eyes, and skin were transferred from dead to living, ova from one uterus to another. Women of sixty gave birth, and face-lifts stopped time on faces. Mylène Demongeot, on TV, was the same lovely doll we'd seen in *Be Beautiful but Shut Up*, preserved intact since 1958.

Our heads spun at the mere thought of cloning, babies carried in artificial wombs, brain implants, sex wearables, completely undifferentiated sexuality. We forgot that, at least for a time, these objects and behaviors would coexist with an older order of things.

The ease of everything still left us briefly stunned and incited people to say of new objects on the market, "Very cool!"

We foresaw that over a lifetime, unimaginable things would appear and people would get used to them, as they had done in so little time with the mobile phone, computer, iPod, and GPS. What disturbed us was the inability to picture our lifestyle in ten years' time, or ourselves perfectly adapted to technologies yet unknown. (Someday, would we be able to see, imprinted on a person's brain, everything they had done, said, seen, and heard?)

We lived in a profusion of everything, objects, information, and "expert opinions." No sooner had an event occurred than someone issued a reflection, whatever the subject: manners of conduct, the body, orgasm, and euthanasia. Everything was discussed and decrypted. Between "addiction," "resilience," and "grief work," there were countless ways of transposing life and emotions into words. Depression, alcoholism, frigidity, anorexia, unhappy childhoods, nothing was lived in vain anymore. The communication of experience and fantasies was pleasing to the conscience. Collective introspection provided models for putting the self into words. The repertoire of shared knowledge grew. The mind grew more agile, children learned at a younger age, and the slowness of school drove young people to distraction. They texted on their mobiles full tilt.

With all the intermingling of concepts, it was increasingly difficult to find a phrase of one's own, the kind that, when silently repeated, helped one live.

On the Internet all one needed do was enter a keyword and thousands of "sites" would leap on the screen. They delivered scraps of sentences and snatches of text that drew us toward other lucky finds in a thrilling treasure hunt. Real gems were thrown back into the infinity of things we hadn't been looking for. It seemed as though we could seize knowledge whole, enter the multiplicity of views flung onto blogs in a new and brutal language. We could research the symptoms of throat cancer, recipes for moussaka, the age of Catherine Deneuve, the weather in Osaka, the growing of hydrangeas and cannabis, the Japanese influence on the development of China—play poker, record films and discs, buy anything from white mice and revolvers to Viagra and dildos, sell and resell them. Talk to strangers, insult and chat them up, invent a self. They were disembodied, voiceless, devoid of odor or gesture; they didn't get under our skin. What mattered was what we could do with them, the law of exchange; pleasure. The great desire for power and impunity was fulfilled. We made our way around a world of objects without subjects. The Internet engineered the dazzling transformation of the world into discourse.

The quick jump-click of the mouse on the screen was the measure of time.

In less than two minutes, one could locate classmates from Camille Jullian high school in Bordeaux, second C2 class, 1980 to 1981, a song by Marie-Josée Neuville, an article from 1988 in *L'Humanité*. The web was the royal road for the remembrance of things past. Archives and all the old things that we'd never even imagined being able to find again arrived with no delay. Memory became inexhaustible, but the depth of time, its sensation conveyed through the odor and yellowing of paper, bent-back pages, paragraphs underscored in an unknown hand, had disappeared. Here we dwelled in the infinite present.

We never stopped wanting to click on "save" and keep all the photos and films, viewable on the spot. Hundreds of images were scattered to the four winds of friendship, a new social use of photos. They were transferred and filed in seldom-opened folders on the computer. What mattered most was the taking of the photos, existence captured and duplicated, recorded as we were living it—cherry trees in bloom, a hotel room in Strasbourg, a baby minutes after birth, places, events, scenes, objects, the complete conservation of life. With digital technology, we drained reality dry.

Our photographs and films—filed by date and viewed onscreen, one after the other without a pause—were pervaded by the light of a time that was unique, no matter how diverse the scenes and landscapes. Another form of past came into being, fluid, with little real memory content. There were too many images for us to stop at each and recall the circumstances in which they were taken. Inside them, we lived a near weightless, transfigured existence. The signs of our existence multiplied and put an end to the sensation of time marching on.

It was strange to think that with DVDs and other media, later generations would know all the most intimate details of our daily lives: our gestures and ways of eating, speaking, and making love; our furniture and underwear. The obscurity of previous centuries would disappear forever, driven away by the camera on a tripod at the photographer's studio, or the digital camera in the bedroom. We were resurrected ahead of time.

And inside ourselves, we had a great, vague memory of the world. Of almost everything we retained little beyond a word, detail, or name that would later make us say, like Georges

Perec, "I remember," whether it concerned Baron Empain's kidnapping, Picorette candies, Bérégovoy's socks, Devaquet, the Falklands War, or the Benco breakfast. But these were not real memories. That was the name we gave them, but in fact they were something quite different: time markers.

The media took charge of the process of memory and forgetting. It commemorated everything that could be commemorated, the appeal of Abbé Pierre, the deaths of Mitterrand and Marguerite Duras, the beginnings and ends of wars, the first step on the moon, Chernobyl, September 11. Every day was the anniversary of something, a law, a crime, the opening of a trial. The media divided time into the yé-yé years, the hippie and the AIDS years. It divided people into generations, De Gaulle, Mitterrand, '68, 'boomers, the digital generation. We belonged to all and none. Our years were nowhere among them.

We were mutating. We didn't know what our new shape would be.

The moon, when we looked up at night, shone fixedly on billions of people, a world whose vastness and teeming activity we could feel inside. Consciousness stretched across the total space of the planet toward other galaxies. The infinite ceased to be imaginary. That is why it seemed inconceivable that one day we would die.

If we tried to enumerate the things that happened outside us, after September 11 we saw a rash of swift-moving events, a series of expectations and fears, interminable times and explosions that paralyzed or deeply distressed us—"nothing will be as it was before" was the dominant theme—and then disappeared, forgotten, unresolved, and commemorated a year or even a month later, as if they were ancient history. There was April 21, the war in Iraq, which fortunately did not include us, and the death of John Paul II, another pope whose name we hadn't retained, let alone his number, the bombing of the Atocha station, the great festive evening for the No vote in the European Constitution referendum, the incendiary nights of rioting in the *banlieue*, Florence Aubenas, the London terrorist attacks, the Lebanon War between Israel and Hezbollah, the Indian Ocean tsunami, Saddam rooted out of a hole and hanged (no one knew when), nebulous epidemics, SARS, avian flu, the chikungunya virus. During the summer that brought the big heat wave, American soldiers were sent home in bags from Iraq, and little old men and women who died from the heat were stacked in refrigeration chambers at the Rungis market.

Everything seemed overwhelming. The United States was the master of time and space, which it occupied according to its needs and interests. Everywhere the rich grew richer and the poor grew poorer. People slept in tents all along the Boulevard Périphérique. The young sneered "Welcome to a world of shit" and briefly rebelled. Only the retired were satisfied, and sought advice on how to save and spend their money, traveled to

Thailand, shopped on eBay, and visited Meetic online dating. Where could revolt come from?

Of all the information we received daily, the most interesting, the kind that mattered most, concerned the next day's weather. The rain-or-shine monitors in the RER stations displayed predictive, almanac-style knowledge that provided us with a daily reason to rejoice or lament, thanks to the surprising and yet invariable factor of weather, whose modification by human activity profoundly shocked us.

It was a nasty speech that hit hard and met with assent from the majority of TV viewers, unperturbed to hear the minister of the interior declare that he wanted to "clean out with a Kärcher pressure washer" the "scum" of the *banlieue*. Traditional values were waved about, order, work, national identity, freighted with threats against enemies that "honest people" were left to identify: the unemployed, suburban youth, illegal immigrants, *sans papiers*, thieves and rapists, etc. Never (or not for a long time) had so few words propagated so much faith, words to which people abandoned themselves, as if made dizzy by all the analyses and data. Disgusted by the seven million poor, the homeless and the unemployment statistics, they put their trust in simplicity. *Of those surveyed, 77 percent say that the legal system is too lenient with offenders.* The old-new philosophers on TV rattled off their stale discourses. Abbé Pierre died, the *Guignols* were still not funny, and

Charlie Hebdo nursed the same old indignations. We sensed that nothing would prevent the election of Sarkozy. Nothing would prevent people's desire from going to term. There was a renewed yearning for servitude and obedience to a leader.

Commercial time invaded calendar time with renewed vigor. Christmas already, people sighed as toys and chocolate besieged the hypermarkets, just after All Saints' weekend. They were depressed, already feeling the vise-grip of the holiday season, which forced one to think of oneself, one's loneliness and purchasing power as compared to the rest of society—as if Christmas night were the crowning moment and end of all existence. It was a vision that made us want to go to sleep in November and wake up in the new year. We entered the most grueling period of desire and hatred of things, the peak of the consumer year. With loathing we stood in overheated lines, and performed the consumer act like a sacrifice, a duty of spending offered up to who-knows-what god in the name of who-knows-what salvation. Resigned to "doing something for Christmas," we bought decorations for the tree and planned the menu for the holiday meal.

In the middle of that first decade of the twenty-first century, which we never referred to as "the noughties," at the table where we'd gathered the children, now getting on forty (though with their jeans and Converse sneakers they still looked like teens), and their partners—the same for several years now— and the grandchildren, and also a man who'd graduated from transitional secret lover to stable companion, eligible for family gatherings, conversation began with a swarm of back-and-forth questions about work, insecure or threatened by downsizing as a result of new ownership, modes of transport, schedules, holidays, how many cigarettes a day and quitting, leisure activities, photo and music downloads, recent purchases of new objects, the latest version of Windows, the latest model of mobile phone, 3G, attitudes toward consumption and time management, everything that helped them refresh their knowledge of one another, assess the other's lifestyle while privately confirming the excellence of their own.

They compared views on films, cross-referenced critics from *Télérama*, *Libération*, *Les Inrocks*, and *Technikart*, expressed enthusiasm for *Six Feet Under* and *24*. They urged us to watch at least one episode, convinced we would do no such thing— wanting to teach us but refusing to be taught, betraying their conviction that our knowledge of things was not as up to speed as theirs.

The talk turned to the upcoming presidential elections and they tried to outdo each other in ridicule of the campaign. They vented their anger at being force-fed Ségo-and-Sarko, mocked the "just order" and "win-win" of the Socialist candidate, her limp and well-reared manner of stringing hollow phrases together. Alarm was expressed at Sarko's populist talent and his irrepressible ascension. People confessed to an inability to choose between Bové, Voynet, and Besancenot, and truth to tell, didn't want to vote for anyone, convinced this election would not be life-changing, though at least one could hope that things would not get worse with Madame the Socialist candidate as president. They finally came around to the great subject of conversation, the media, its manipulation of public opinion and the ways of getting around it. None could be believed but YouTube, Wikipedia, Rezo.net, Acrimed on the web. The critique of media mattered more than the information itself.

All was derision and gleeful festive fatalism. The *banlieue* would blaze again, the Israeli-Palestinian conflict was incurable. The planet was headed for disaster with global warming, the melting of the polar ice caps and the death of bees. Someone exclaimed "And your point is?" and then "What about avian flu?" and "Is Ariel Sharon still in a coma?" This sparked an enumeration of other forgotten things—SARS, the Clearstream affair, the anti-unemployment movements—whose object was less to acknowledge collective amnesia than castigate media control of the imagination. The disappearance of the most recent past was stupefying.

There was no memory or narration, only recollections of the 1970s, which seemed desirable to those of us who had been there and those who had been very young, and remembered only objects, TV programs, music, iron-on knee patches, Kiri the Clown, the slot-load portable record player, Travolta and *Saturday Night Fever*.

In all this lively exchange, no one had the patience to tell stories.

We listened, quietly interjected, mindful to play the role of moderator and prevent the "add-on" guests from being left out. We placed ourselves above the collusion of couples and family members, careful to divert the stirrings of discord. We were tolerant of teasing about our ignorance of technology and felt ourselves become the indulgent ageless chief of a uniformly adolescent tribe. We did not yet fully grasp that we were a grandparent, as if this title was forever reserved for our own grandparents, for a sort of essence that their deaths had done nothing to alter.

Once again, amidst the closely packed bodies, the passing of hors d'oeuvres and foie gras, chewing and jokes and avoidance of serious subjects, the immaterial reality of the holiday meal was built. It was a reality whose strength and density we felt when we escaped a moment to smoke a cigarette, or check the turkey, then returned to the buzzing table to find ourselves a stranger to the new conversation. We felt that something of childhood was being replayed, an age-old golden scene: people sitting at a table, blurred faces, voices talking all at once.

After coffee, they settled with gusto in front of the TV and installed the new Nintendo console and the Wii. They played virtual tennis and boxing, shouting and swearing and hurling themselves about in front of the screen. The smaller children played hide-and-seek in all the rooms, abandoning the gifts from the day before, which lay scattered on the floor. We returned to the table to cool down with a Perrier or a Coke. Silences foretold an imminent disbanding. We looked at the clock. We emerged from holiday meal time, which had no minute or second hands. Toys and stuffed animals were gathered up with all the nursery paraphernalia that accompanied every visit. After the effusions and thanks upon departure came the orders to the children to give us a kiss, and the circular questioning "We haven't forgotten anything, have we?" The private worlds of couples re-formed and dispersed in their respective cars. Silence descended. We removed the leaf from the table, started the dishwasher, and retrieved a piece of doll clothing from under a chair. We recognized the weary plenitude of having once again "been a good hostess," harmoniously navigated all the stages of a rite in which we were now the oldest mainstay.

In this photo, selected from hundreds contained in Photo Service envelopes or stored in computer files, a middle-aged woman with reddish-blonde hair and a black low-cut sweater sits in a big multicolored armchair, tipped almost all the way back, with her arms around a little girl. The girl wears jeans and a pale green zip-front sweater. She sprawls across the woman's legs, one of which is visible, sheathed in black nylon. The two faces are close together at slightly different levels. The woman's is pale with flushed patches that appear after meals, a little gaunt, with fine lines on the forehead. She smiles. The child is olive-skinned with big serious brown eyes. She is saying something. The only similarity between them is rumpled hair of identical length. A few strands, swept to the front, mingle on their necks. The woman's hands in the foreground, the joints pronounced, almost gnarled, appear oversized. Her smile, her way of staring into the lens and holding the child express an attitude that is less one of possession than of offering, as one might see in a photo of generational transfer—grandmother presents granddaughter, an establishment of filiation. The bookshelves in the background are streaked with light reflected by the plastic-covered spines of the Pléiades. Two names stand out, Pavese, Elfriede Jelinek. The traditional decor of an intellectual, who keeps the books separate from the other cultural media, DVDs, videocassettes, CDs, as if for her, the latter belonged to a separate, perhaps less dignified realm. Written on the back of the photo, *Cergy, December 25, 2006.*

She is the woman in the picture. When she looks at it, she can say with a high degree of certainty, insofar as the face in the photo and her face of the present are not noticeably different, that nothing further has been lost of what will eventually be gone for good (but when and how this will happen, she prefers not to think about). This is me = I see no additional signs of aging. But she doesn't think about those signs either, and generally lives in denial—not of her age, which is sixty-six, but of what it represents for the very young. She feels no age difference with women of forty-five or fifty, an illusion which the latter destroy in the course of conversation, without malice but implying that she doesn't belong to the same generation as they, and is seen by them in the way she herself sees a woman of eighty, i.e., old. Unlike adolescence, when she was sure of not being the same from one year or even one month to the next, now she feels immutable in a world that moves ahead in leaps and bounds. Although between the photo from the beach at Trouville and the one from Christmas 2006, a number of events have occurred. If we omit details such as the degree and duration of upheaval surrounding each, and the causal relations that may have existed between them, the list appears as follows:

—the breakup with the man she called the young man, a separation she slowly, secretively, and tenaciously pursued, and which became irrevocable one Saturday in September 1999, when she watched a fish, a tench he'd just pulled from the water, thrash and jerk on the grass for minutes before it died, and which she ate with him that evening in disgust

—her retirement, which had for so long been the most distant point she could imagine in future time, as menopause had once been. Overnight, the course materials she'd created and the reading notes she'd used to prepare them ceased to have a purpose. For lack of use, the scholarly language she'd acquired was erased inside her, and now when she seeks and does not find the name for a figure of rhetoric, she is forced to say, as her mother once had about a flower whose name escaped her, "I used to know what that was called"

—jealousy vis-à-vis the young man's new middle-aged partner, as if it were necessary to occupy the time freed by retirement, or become "young" again through romantic torment he'd never caused her to feel when they were together, a jealousy she groomed for weeks on end, like a new career, until the only thing she wanted was to be rid of it

—a tumor of the kind that seems to burgeon in the breasts of all women her age, and appeared to her a normal occurrence, almost, because the things we most fear, happen. At the same time, she received the news that a baby was growing in the womb of her eldest son's partner—the ultrasound revealed a girl, and meanwhile she'd lost all her hair as a result of chemotherapy. This replacement of herself in the world, with no delay, profoundly disturbed her

—in the period between the confirmation of a birth and her own possible death, she met a younger man, who attracted her with his gentleness and his penchant for everything that makes one dream, books, music, films. This miraculous coincidence gave her a chance to triumph over death through love and eroticism, and continued later as an affair in separate residences, an alternation of presence and absence, the only scheme that suited them and their difficulty to be, and not to be, together

—the death at sixteen of the black-and-white cat of common species, who had returned after years of quaking fat to the frailty of the photo from the winter of 1992. She covered the cat with earth from the garden during the heat wave while the neighbors jumped screaming into their pool. With this gesture that she had never performed before she felt as if she were burying all the people in her life who had died, her parents, the last aunt on her mother's side, the older man who'd been her first lover after the divorce, and had remained a friend and died of a heart attack two summers earlier—a burial that foreshadowed her own.

These events, happy or sad, when she compares them to others that happened longer ago, do not at all seem to have modified her ways of thinking, tastes, or interests, which became settled when she was about fifty in a kind of inner solidification. The series of gaps that separate all the past versions of herself ends there. What has most changed in her is the perception of time and her own location within it. And so she realizes with amazement that back at the time when she was asked to do dictations from Colette at school, the author was still alive, and that her own grandmother, who was twelve when Victor Hugo died, must have had a day off school on account of the funeral (but by then she already worked in the fields, no doubt). And while the loss of her parents grows more and more distant in time (twenty and forty years ago now), and nothing in her way of living or thinking resembles theirs (indeed hers would "make them turn over in their graves"), she feels she is drawing closer to them. As the time ahead objectively decreases, the time behind her stretches farther and farther back, to long before birth, and ahead to a time after her death. She imagines people saying, perhaps in thirty or forty years, that she was alive for the Algerian War, just as they used to say of her great-grandparents "they were alive for the War of 1870."

She has lost her sense of the future, a kind of limitless background on which her actions and gestures were once projected, a waiting for all the good and unknown things that lived inside her as she walked up Boulevard de la Marne to the university in the fall, or finished the last page of *The Mandarins*, and, years later, jumped into the Austin Mini after class to fetch the children, and even later, after her divorce and the death of her mother, left for the United States for the first time with *L'Amerique* by Joe Dassin playing in her head, and up until three years ago, when she threw a coin into the Trevi Fountain and made a wish to return to Rome.

The future is replaced by a sense of urgency that torments her. She is afraid that as she ages her memory will become cloudy and silent, as it was in her first years of life, which she won't remember anymore. Already when she tries to recall her colleagues from the lycée in the mountains where she taught for two years, she sees silhouettes and faces, some with extreme precision, but she cannot possibly "put a name to them." She tries desperately to retrieve the missing name, match the name with the person, join the separate halves. Maybe one day all things and their names will slip out of alignment and she'll no longer be able to put words to reality. All that will remain is the reality that cannot be spoken. Now's the time to give *form* to her future absence through writing, start the book, still a draft of thousands of notes, which has doubled her existence for the past twenty years and is thus obliged to cover a longer and longer time.

She's given up trying to deduce this form that is able to contain her life from the sensation she has on the beach with her eyes closed or in a hotel room, that sense of replicating herself and physically existing in several places she's known over her life, and thus attaining a palimpsest time. So far, the sensation has not taken her anywhere in writing or any field of knowledge. Like the minutes after orgasm, it creates the desire to write, nothing more. And somehow, by erasing words, images, objects, people, it prefigures if not death, then the state she'll be in one day, sinking, as the very old do, into the contemplation of trees, sons and grandchildren (her view of them quite blurred due to "age-related macular degeneration"), stripped of learning and history, her own and that of the world, or afflicted with Alzheimer's, unable to name the day, month, or season.

What matters to her, on the contrary, is to seize this time that comprises her life on Earth at a given period, the time that has coursed through her, the world she has recorded merely by living. She has mined her intuition of what her book's form will be from another sensation, the one that engulfs her when, starting with a frozen memory-image of herself with other kids on a hospital bed after tonsil surgery, after the war, or crossing Paris on a bus in July of '68, she seems to melt into an indistinct whole whose parts she manages to pull free, one at a time, through an effort of critical consciousness: elements of herself, customs, gestures, words, etc. The tiny moment of the past grows and opens onto a horizon, at once mobile and uniform in tone, of one or several years. Then, in a state of profound, almost dazzling satisfaction, she finds something that the image from personal memory doesn't give her on its own: a kind of vast collective sensation that takes her consciousness, her entire being, into itself. She has the same feeling, alone in the car on the highway, of being *taken into* the indefinable whole of the world of now, from the closest to the most remote of things.

So her book's form can only emerge from her complete immersion in the images from her memory in order to identify, with relative certainty, the specific signs of the times, the years to which the images belong, gradually linking them to others; to try to hear the words people spoke, what they said about events and things, skim it off the mass of floating speech, that *hubbub* that tirelessly ferries the wordings and rewordings of what we are and what we must be, think, believe, fear, and hope. All that the world has impressed upon her and her contemporaries she will use to reconstitute a common time, the one that made its way through the years of the distant past and glided all the way to the present. By retrieving the memory of collective memory in an individual memory, she will capture the lived dimension of History.

This will not be a work of remembrance in the usual sense, aimed at putting a life into story, creating an explanation of self. She will go within herself only to retrieve the world, the memory and imagination of its bygone days, grasp the changes in ideas, beliefs, and sensibility, the transformation of people and the subject that she has seen—perhaps nothing compared to those her granddaughter will see, as will all beings who are alive in 2070. To hunt down sensations that are already there, as yet unnamed, such as the one that is making her write.

It will be a slippery narrative composed in an unremitting

continuous tense, absolute, devouring the present as it goes, all the way to the final image of a life. An outpouring, but suspended at regular intervals by photos and scenes from films that capture the successive body shapes and social positions of her being—freeze-frames on memories, and at the same time reports on the development of her existence, the things that have made it singular, not because of the nature of the elements of her life, whether external (social trajectory, profession) or internal (thoughts and aspirations, the desire to write), but because of their combinations, each unique unto itself. To this "incessantly not-she" of photos will correspond, in mirror image, the "she" of writing.

There is no "I" in what she views as a sort of impersonal autobiography. There is only "one" and "we," as if now it were her turn to tell the story of the time-before.

In the old days, when she tried to write in her student room, she yearned to find an unknown language that would unveil mysterious things, in the way of a clairvoyant. She also imagined the finished book as a revelation to others of her innermost being, a superior achievement, a kind of glory. She would have given anything to "become a writer," in the same way that she had longed as a child to wake up as Scarlett O'Hara one morning. Later, as she stood in grueling classes of forty students, or pushed a shopping cart at the supermarket, or sat on a bench in the public gardens next to a baby carriage, those dreams deserted her. There was no ineffable world that leapt out from inspired words, as if by magic, and she would never write except from inside her language, which is everyone's language, the only tool she's ever intended on using to act upon the things that outraged her. So the book to be written represented an instrument of struggle. She hasn't abandoned this ambition. But now, more than anything, she would like to capture the light that suffuses faces that can no longer be seen and tables groaning with vanished food, the light that was already present in the stories of Sundays in childhood and has continued to settle upon things from the moment they are lived, a light from before. Save

—the little village fête at Bazoches-sur-Hoëne with the bumper cars

—the hotel room on the rue Beauvoisine in Rouen, not far from the Lepouzé bookstore, where Cayatte filmed a scene for *To Die of Love*

—the wine tap at the Carrefour on rue du Parmelan, Annecy

—*I leaned against the beauty of the world / And I held the smell of the seasons in my hands*

—the merry-go-round at the spa park, in Saint-Honoré-les Bains

—the very young woman in a red coat walking down the sidewalk next to a staggering man she had gone to fetch at the Café Le Duguesclin, in the winter, in La Roche-Posay

—the film *People of No Importance*

—the half-torn poster for the dating site 3615 Ulla at the bottom of the hill in Fleury-sur-Andelle

—a bar and a jukebox that played *Apache* at Tally Ho Corner, Finchley

—a house at the very back of a garden, 35 avenue Edmond Rostand in Villiers-le-Bel

—the gaze of the black-and-white cat the moment the needle put her to sleep

—the man in pajamas and slippers who wept every afternoon in the lobby of the old folks' home in Pontoise, and asked visitors to call his son, holding up a piece of soiled paper on which a phone number was written

—the woman of the Bentalha massacre in Algeria in the photo by Hocine that resembles a Pietà

—the dazzling sun on the walls of San Michele Cemetery, seen from the shade of the Fondamenta Nuove

Save something from the time where we will never be again.

TRANSLATOR'S NOTE

The Years is at least twice as long as all but one of AE's previous books and in other ways, too, is a departure from her other work. There are many different atmospheres and registers, styles and rhythms. It is a book with a vast, sweeping scope (from microcosm to macrocosm and back), lots of movement and many different "speeds."

The book is punctuated by scenes of holiday meals—long, animated afternoons with family and friends. They provide a concentrated view of where the "characters" are in their lives and in history. They begin shortly after the narrator's birth in 1940 until her sixty-sixth year.

During the holiday meals of the narrator's childhood, when the parents and their friends and their own parents were alive, the talk is of hardship in their early lives and the world wars. The elders tell stories, conjure up ancestors and distant cousins and long-ago neighbors. The children (including the narrator) go off to play together and then return to the table for dessert. They listen to the adults talk, sing (war songs, love songs), and tell the "two great narratives: the story of war and the story of origins."

The narrator says of this generation, that of the parents and earlier:

From a common ground of hunger and fear, everything was told in the "we."

This sets the scene for the narrator/writer's own "project" to speak in a "*je* collectif."

She writes about the years between 1940 and 2007 as if the story were not only hers but that of her generation.

To write in the "*je* collectif," in French AE uses the *nous* or the *on* (which I translate mostly as "we" but sometimes as "one" for formality or rhythm or simply because it is the only choice that presents itself; very occasionally I use the impersonal "you"). She also uses *ils/elles* (they) or *les gens* (people), and later in the paragraph switches pronouns, often more than once (*on, nous, ils* . . .). Each pronoun clearly refers to the same subject or subjects. In French it is quite striking, and presents a certain translation challenge. The shifts imply that "we" and "one" (that is, *nous* and *on*) contain an "I" or a "them," a "her," "him," and "you," a "someone" or "some people"—truly *collectif*!

It is very common in French to English translation, in sentences where the subject is *on*, to translate into the passive voice. I know the passive voice can be windy and unwieldy, but in *The Years*, it is sometimes appropriate to use it in order to maintain the impersonal tone.

Another recurring element in the book is the description of photos (or home movies or video segments) from different times in the narrator's life.

Here is her own description of their function in her narrative:

[These are] freeze-frames on memories, and at the same time reports on the development of her existence, the things

that have made it singular, not because of the nature of the elements of her life, whether external (social trajectory, profession) or internal (thoughts and aspirations, the desire to write), but because of their combinations, each unique unto itself. *To this "incessantly not-she" of photos will correspond, in mirror image, the "she" of writing.* (emphasis added)

The actual descriptions of the photos are accompanied by the author's speculations on what "the girl in the photo," Annie, might be thinking (how she views world events, if at all; and especially how she views herself and her future).

The descriptions of the photos are generally precise in clear-cut prose.

However, the speculations are sometimes written in other styles: sinuous as she drifts from one memory to the next, or telegraphic as she makes mental lists of things seen and lived (some she'd rather forget), movies, books, songs . . .

Yet another thread in the book (which comes with its own style and translation challenges) is the book in progress—*the* book, *this* book, the one that becomes *The Years*. She reflects upon it for decades, takes copious notes, and endlessly seeks a form for her book. She goes back to former times of her life, to "selves" superimposed on one another, alludes to a sensation she calls "a palimpsest sensation." She waits for a catalyst event or image—a madeleine à la Proust. In this sense, we witness a kind of *mise en abyme* in the making (the narrator compares the book-to-come to Dorothea Tanning's painting *Birthday*). Toward the end, when she is getting closer and closer to starting, this is how she describes the book-to-come:

> *It will be a slippery narrative, composed in an unremitting continuous tense, absolute, devouring the present as it goes,* all the way to the final image of a life. An outpouring, but suspended at regular intervals by photos and scenes from films . . .
> There is no "I" in what she views as a sort of impersonal autobiography. There is only "one" and "we," as if now it were her turn to tell the story of the time-before. (emphasis added)

Early in the process, I vastly reduced the use of the continuous tense, and shortened many sentences, at the suggestion of my editor at Seven Stories. I don't think this "unremitting continuous tense" has to be, or can be, literally applied in the entire book, but there are places where it could be considered the model for the writing (and the translation). For instance, this sense of continuity and "devouring the present" is captured in sequences of long sentences where the writing takes off like a shot. There are sentences that go on for entire paragraphs. It is often the case in the holiday dinner scenes. After reducing the length of some marathon sentences for clarity, I restored all that I could to their full "breathless" length, with considerable help from commas and dashes. AE's "breathless" marathon sentences sometimes give the impression that time is speeding up. Time in the book slows down, speeds up, sweeps us away, repeats itself, grinds to a halt, or transforms into a very intricately detailed interior time. The narrative shrinks and expands constantly, and these effects are shored up by sentence structure, verb tense, mode, and so on.

In translating *The Years* there was a balance to maintain between the plain, incisive writing (*écriture plate*), so often associated with the author's work, and a prose more sinuous and expansive.

There were times to be terse and times to be sweeping.

Is this Ernaux's *Remembrance of Things Past* (or her *Gone with the Wind*, *Life and Fate*, with perhaps a nod to Virginia Woolf: the stream of consciousness, the struggle with the "I" . . . ?

I have added a few footnotes. I had to look up quite a number of names, and incidents, which would perhaps be clear to many French readers but not to every English reader.

As in all of Ernaux's books, it is worthwhile to pay attention to the spacing between sections. There is method in it.

—Alison L. Strayer
Paris, April 2017

Born in 1940, ANNIE ERNAUX grew up in Normandy, studied at Rouen University, and began teaching high school. From 1977 to 2000, she was a professor at the Centre National d'Enseignement par Correspondance. One of France's most esteemed living writers, her books have been subject to much critical acclaim. She won the prestigious Prix Renaudot for *A Man's Place* when it was first published in French in 1984. The English edition was a *New York Times* Notable Book and a finalist for the *Los Angeles Times* Book Prize. The English edition of *A Woman's Story* was a *New York Times* Notable Book.

ALISON L. STRAYER is a Canadian writer and translator. Her work has been shortlisted for the Governor General's Award for Literature and for Translation, the Grand Prix du livre de Montréal, and the Prix littéraire France-Québec. She lives in Paris

About Seven Stories Press

SEVEN STORIES PRESS is an independent book publisher based in New York City. We publish works of the imagination by such writers as Nelson Algren, Russell Banks, Octavia E. Butler, Ani DiFranco, Assia Djebar, Ariel Dorfman, Coco Fusco, Barry Gifford, Martha Long, Luis Negrón, Hwang Sok-yong, Lee Stringer, and Kurt Vonnegut, to name a few, together with political titles by voices of conscience, including Subhankar Banerjee, the Boston Women's Health Collective, Noam Chomsky, Angela Y. Davis, Human Rights Watch, Derrick Jensen, Ralph Nader, Loretta Napoleoni, Gary Null, Greg Palast, Project Censored, Barbara Seaman, Alice Walker, Gary Webb, and Howard Zinn, among many others. Seven Stories Press believes publishers have a special responsibility to defend free speech and human rights, and to celebrate the gifts of the human imagination, wherever we can. In 2012 we launched Triangle Square books for young readers with strong social justice and narrative components, telling personal stories of courage and commitment. For additional information, visit www.sevenstories.com.